Sit or Stand 2.0

Living Successfully Beyond Your Shadows

Cory George

Published by:

PO Box 813
Riverdale, MD 20738

Sit or Stand, 2.0: Living Successfully Beyond Your Shadows

Copyright © 2015 by Cory George Media

Photography and Cover Layout: Travis Long for TRAPHIX

No part of this book may be reproduced or transmitted in any form or by any means without written permission of the author.

All rights reserved.

ISBN 978-0-578-16785-5

Manufactured in the United States of America

The new iteration of this work is dedicated to some very special people that are now tenants of the highest of places.

My Super Women: Audrey Louise George (Big Mama), Brenda Gayle George Williams (Aunt Brenda/Mom), Gertie Mae Warren (Aunt Mae): Your undying love, attention, affection, and attendance in my life will never go without notice. You loved me when even when I couldn't put all of the pieces together.

Victor Roy George: God saw fit to take you sooner than we all expected. Your absence somehow brought us closer together as a family and was the catalyst for conversations that we may have never found the courage to have which means that your life had at least one purpose. You will forever be my baby brother and I know that your heart and mind are at peace.

Russell Wayne George, Sr.: Through the word of God I've learned that love is patient and love is kind…most importantly, love forgives all. Dad, our relationship was always one that was constantly on the hot seat but during your last days you reconciled it all in ways I didn't know that I needed. My wish is that you are now at spiritual and physical peace from all the "brokenness" that existed before my existence. I indeed loved you despite everything. Say hi to Big Mama, Aunt Brenda, Aunt Mae, Uncle Victor, and your baby boy, Victor Roy.

ACKNOWLEDGMENTS

God: Thank you for the renewable grace and mercy that you bestow upon my life at the start of each beautiful and blessed day. Also, I thank you for the purpose placed upon my life and for every carefully-planned experience that was designed for my benefit and those that I hope to inspire to live out loud. I graciously accept your will and the assignments over my life. You loved me first and will love me last. Being created in your image empowers, motivates, and fuels my journey and forces me to stop and recalibrate when necessary. May you continue to cover all of the steps that pave this journey that you have planned for the rest of my life.

I give God complete thanks for the absolute loves of my life; my sons, Tyler and Justin. Thank you for loving me unconditionally. I want nothing more than for you to be beautiful examples of love, courage, wisdom, respect, and grace. Being your father is the most gratifying job I will ever have and I am honored to be the best I can for you.

Lastly, I give special thanks to everyone who has played a part in this continuing journey. If you've committed a trespass against me I have forgiven you as I hope you have forgiven me. If you've supported me I pray that I can continue to support you in return. Love is in the details…and I'm still writing them.

To those who remain voiceless, nameless, and uncounted as a result of childhood sexual abuse: Your pain is not suffered in vain and your voice is as important as anyone else's. I pray that you one day learn to trust the power of your Godly-bestowed voice.

Table of Contents

Prologue		7
Chapter 1	In The Beginning	14
Chapter 2	Accepting Your Truth: Letting the Smoke Clear	34
Chapter 3	Depression: The Darkness That Blocked My Light	46
Chapter 4	Paving the Way for Inner Peace	56
Chapter 5	The Power & Freedom of Forgiveness	68
Chapter 6	Imperfection: God's Perfect Fingerprint	93
Chapter 7	Who's Loving YOU?	107
Chapter 8	From Desires to Deservedness	131
Chapter 9	The Truth About Expectations	141
Chapter 10	The Purge: Lose to Win	154
Chapter 11	Self-Marketing 101	168
Chapter 12	Recognizing and Building Your Support System	179
Chapter 13	Planning for Success: Planning For Life	190
Chapter 14	Driving Beyond the Stop Signs	207
Chapter 15	Walking a Mile in Aunt Brenda's Shoes	217
Chapter 16	Paying it Forward & Defining Your Legacy	229
Capstone Questionnaire		239
Final Thoughts & Wishes		244
About Cory George, MS, CAMS-I, CDVS-I		245

PROLOGUE

Five years has passed since the initial release of *Sit or Stand*. Life has made room for more valuable experiences than I expected. Yet, the one question that has always existed in the midst of each experience was always "Do I **SIT** quietly and take whatever is dispensed to me without question or do I take a **STAND** and declare my right to a more meaningful life based on the foundations of respect (for myself, my fellow man, and the universe), growth, and the willingness to learn at every turn?" Sometimes, the answer wasn't so obvious but an answer was always necessary. This process involved many stops, restarts, and detours along the way. At times I felt elated to be blessed with the ability to share a newfound gem of knowledge. At other I was completely overwhelmed by the lessons I was forced to learn. Tears of pain and joy were shed as a part of my personal mental detoxification process. Those tears were usually followed by a simple "thank you, Jesus" because many times I wondered why I hadn't decided to "check out" of this existence. Sooner or later, the reasons were revealed and it was those same reasons that gave more strength to the testimonies I decided to share throughout this book.

I subtitled the book *Living Successfully Beyond Your Shadows* because, like shadows, some of life's most harrowing issues becomes attached to one's spirit and shows up at any moment based on the level of control that we have over those issues. Future relationships, projects, and career moves can be severely hampered or totally destroyed as a result of an unstable spirit. The resurfacing of the issues in question can cast a haze upon one's "emotional vision" and can also drastically affect how one interprets everything that comes afterwards. The interpretations usually lean towards being more negative and stifling. Therefore, one's reaction is more than likely going to be more negative than expected. We cannot deny the effects and level of control that our issues currently exhibit over our lives but we can learn how to fully interpret and better manage the effects and gain more control and as a result, bring more peace to our existence. An additional benefit is that our life choices become more favorable to what we require to sustain joy and peace of mind. Finally, we eventually become more honest with ourselves as it relates to who we are, why certain events and people affect us in a particular way and what we bring to each table at which we sit.

In mentioning the word "table" I am referring to the different relationships or situations in which we are present and held accountable for our means of interacting. It can range from a familial connection to a business relationship. It can also include the relationship you have with yourself which, at times, can be the toughest relationship to maintain. By understanding and taking full ownership of what you are capable of providing at different times allows you to make commitments that you are more than likely to uphold. In turn, the fulfillment of these expectations will also result in more trust extended to you. Also, you are able to ask of others exactly what you can honestly provide in return. Your connections will become stronger and more opportunities may become available because you will be viewed as someone who can live up to specific expectations required of specific opportunities.

I'm sure you're wondering if this particular book is for you. I want you to take a look at the questions listed below:

- Is it difficult for you to accept my past as a part of living honestly and authentically?
- Is it difficult for you to envision a successful future for yourself as a result of particularly damaging life events?
- Is a lack of forgiveness keeping you captive in a place filled with anger, resentment, depression, and self-inflicted isolation?
- Do you have an extreme need for validation and approval?
- Is your level of self-esteem fostering unhealthy or otherwise risky behaviors?

- Taking your immediate social circle into consideration, do you feel less supported in your desires to improve your quality of life?
- Is your inability to overcome your past hurt hampering your ability to maintain healthy romantic relationships?
- Do you often feel victimized?

If you answered yes to at least three of the questions listed above then this book may serve as a starting point in your efforts to recapture the resilience that has always been a part of your total being. There is an opportunity to remove most of the clouds so that your vision is less-influenced by yesterday's troubles. Today's work towards your personal freedom will vastly sharpen your ability to foresee a future that is less monotone so that the forecast for your own life is more vivid and positively detailed. You will find that your goals will become less influenced by your need to merely survive and more influenced by your need to thrive. The energy resulting from your behavior will begin to positively influence others; most often without you having to say a word. Your actions, and not your promises, will be the gage by which people measure their ability to trust you.

Experiences come a dime a dozen and no one is afforded the opportunity to live without them. However, there comes a time when a decision must be made as to how each experience will continue to affect our movement in this world and how these experiences will continue to affect our relationships with others. As time progresses it will be discovered that some of our most soul and spirit-wrenching experiences serve as the backdrop for revelation of destiny and purpose. The increased empathy that is developed as a direct result of pain and suffering is at the base of mostly everything we deem purposeful and rewarding. Empathy also allows us to connect to others in ways that money or any type of impersonal bestowment can ever leverage because the brother/sister hood is found in the experiences that are shared and/or witnessed. The sooner one comes to understand that EVERYONE has had to face some type of adversity is the sooner that the feeling of being totally alone becomes less realistic.

It is safe to assume that everyone desires to attain a certain level of happiness and contentment that leads to a life more fulfilled and purposeful. My desired quality of life will likely not be the same as desired by someone standing beside me so it is imperative that we understand ourselves well enough to know what we want, to become deserving of what we desire, and learn how to maintain the drive that is required in order for us strive for whatever it is that we desire. We must also come to a point where we accept our life as it has already occurred, both good and not so good, in hopes of unearthing valuable lessons that are waiting to be discovered. In turn, you will become more highly self-aware and are better able to determine what, and who, is required to help sustain a certain level of joy. The fear of holding one's self accountable becomes less of a daunting task and more of a welcomed process because the desire to become better as a result of every experience will outweigh the fear of uncovering yet another detail that requires more work.

For years I struggled with extreme self-doubt, low self-esteem, and a poor sense of self-worth. As a result I was plagued with indecisiveness and crippled by bad choices. On one hand I knew exactly what I wanted but I lacked a credible plan of action because it was riddled with unrealistic expectations and a high level of dependency on external people and objects. I finally came to the understanding that my indecisiveness was causing me to make choices that had a direct effect on my quality of life. Then, I became resigned to the fact that my life was just what it was, filled with incomplete goals, unresolved issues, and a string of decisions that were self-destructive and not conducive to the level of happiness that everyone felt I deserved. The problems remained because I had yet to believe in my true right to joy and prosperity as others had believed and the promise that God had always had for my life. For years my goal was to simply survive and do it all over again the next day. I settled for relationships that were "easy" to manage but brought nothing in terms of growth, stability or true comfort. I also settled for jobs that were just jobs. I also had knowingly settled for family members who spoke negatively about me behind my back but smiled to my face while knowing that they had no idea of the pain, guilt, and shame that I harbored. I also settled for the dark secrets that cloaked my lineage for what seemed like generations. In blatant terms, I settled for life as it was, unrewarding and disjointed.

This book is by no means a call for participants of a pity party. Instead, it is a celebration call for every individual that is ready to come out of hiding and unearth their true identity, facing difficulty reconciling imperfections against talents and gifts, and perhaps finding it impossible to believe that some of their darkest hours are meant to reveal their ultimate life purpose. It is also a declaration of life that is finally recognized as a personalized gift from God. He has specific plans for your life that only YOU can accomplish. He has equipped you with a personal power that, when combined with grace and favor, becomes a superpower that only you can yield. That same superpower will aid you during the downturns that WILL happen and command you to bless others with the lessons learned on the roads you will have traveled.

God promised us a life of prosperity (wealth, health and other areas of our lives) so it is important for each of us to understand that the promise also comes with the resources to make it possible. When one learns how to properly utilize those resources in a way that fortifies one's resident abilities then the breakthroughs will manifest. You can't learn to ride a bicycle without a bicycle nor can you write a book without a single word. Yet, when you place yourself in the driver's seat you are able to harness the power of each resource for your benefit instead of letting the resource dictate your movement. Expectations become more reasonable and attainable therefore resulting in less disappointment. Harnessing this resident power doesn't magically shift the universe into a tilt in your favor. Some downturns are inevitable because, as I will discuss more than once throughout the book, some events and scenarios are out of your region of control. The sooner that this fact is accepted one is able to create a path to reconciliation and, if necessary, forgiveness.

We should not use insurmountable situations as a barometer for measuring self-worth. It is the trick that keeps us at a supposed safe level of existence. But being safe isn't always good. Neither is only doing what is comfortable always comforting. When we become comfortable with pain, defeat, and failure we begin writing our own prescription for a myriad of bad choices. The effects of these choices can be very dangerous and may very well cost you or someone else their life. So long as we believe that we have nothing else to gain or offer the world we will continue the cycle of self-inflicted agony and at some point begin to blame others for the inability to react rationally and make wise decisions. We can only blame others for so long before we MUST take credit for allowing ourselves to remain in a space of despair. I explain the tools that assisted me in taking control of my life and dictating my own level of success and failure. In addition, it is my desire that the reader understands that they have the same right to joy and prosperity as the next person.

We are all independent beings that must learn how to become safely codependent upon others in a way that promotes betterment for all parties involved. We sometimes forget that our goals and desires usually require at least one other person or resource to come to fruition. But the level of work and commitment required by all parties can become blurred and confusing if one does not hold on to a sense of responsibility to self; becoming more of an independent figure instead of one that is motivated and dictated by every external action being presented. This concept can be applied to relationships with family, friends, coworkers, acquaintances and the personal and most revealing relationship you have with yourself. Each one of these relationships are different but are rooted upon the same fundamental principle of mutual benefit. Bettering yourself will inject betterment into all of your other relationships and vice versa. Learning to capitalize on the lessons of others may also afford you the opportunity not to repeat mistakes made by others. Also, improving your resilience to withstand most of the rough moments and increasing your compassion for life that exists around you must begin with a selfish desire to satisfy your need to feel complete without confirmation from an extreme amount of external sources.

Before you begin this journey I request that you repeat the following oath out loud at least twice:

- I vow to trust that GOD has his hands placed upon my shoulder at all times
- I vow to force myself to smile in the face of adversity and confusion
- I vow to move out of the way of my own advancement
- I vow to speak and think kindly of myself so that I may truthfully do the same for others
- I vow to welcome ALL of the lessons that all of my experiences WILL bring
- I vow to love because it is the RIGHT thing to do despite my experiences
- I vow to be adamant about the respect I expect to receive from others
- I vow to learn to trust my own voice even when it is seemingly shaky
- I vow to always believe that I am exceptional despite external opinion and criticism
- I vow to recognize the positive impact of and perform acts kindness
- I vow to never resist listening, learning, applying, and living
- I vow to remember that I was created ON PURPOSE therefore I am PURPOSE-FILLED

CHAPTER 1

IN THE BEGINNING

> ***PERSONAL PLEDGE:*** *I understand that every story has a beginning and it is that fact alone that connects us all. The easiest way to begin to help myself is to acknowledge all parts of my story. This acknowledgement will provide the clarity required to address my issues as openly and honestly as possible.*

It is my strong opinion that most personality traits that we exhibit as adults are tightly connected to the types of resolutions, or lack thereof, to issues faced throughout early childhood, adolescent, and teen years. Our emotional DNA, which is highly influenced by attributes such as familial ties, cultural influences and environmental factors, has an extraordinary influence on what we later decide is "normal". The acceptance of what is considered normal becomes the baseline by which all of life's occurrences are measured. By means of habit we adopt specific philosophies handed down to us by our parents, caregivers, and others that we view as highly influential even if those philosophies haven't resulted in optimal results for the same people that bestowed them upon us. These philosophies can be considered modes of operation. Examples can include how one decides to deal with specific family issues, the level of privacy practiced within a family system, the level and type of engagement towards one another, as well as our chosen methods of healing (if any).

I felt it was appropriate to begin this journey by sharing the roots of my beginnings as a way to show the importance of acknowledging where everything starts. It is also important to understand how much one's past can control an untold future, especially if you rely on your past as the ONLY metric to measure what you may expect in your future. Most times, these records become very blurred or otherwise forgotten as we traverse through our daily lives and we tend to believe that if we are able to forget it then we are able to live our lives without any residual effects. Hopefully, you will be inspired to acknowledge your own beginnings and understand that these events help you understand how and why you have become who you are up to this point. I used to be afraid and ashamed to tell these stories but now I offer them to you because I am human just as is everyone that stands in front of you, beside you, and behind you. I had to learn the hard way that we all have a unique place and purpose in this world. Hopefully, you will gain the same knowledge sooner rather than later.

Growing up for me was at times extremely joyous as well as extremely painful and exhausting. I was the first born of my mother and father's three children together. At the time of my birth my mother and father were married and were nineteen and twenty years old, respectively. My mother, in my opinion, got married as a rite of passage as an adult instead of the institution itself. We lived in Houston, Texas during my youngest years and we seemed to have it all. At least that's what I believed in the early years of my life. But, sometimes people grow apart or they grow up and realize that their life wasn't going the way that they had anticipated. My earliest memories of my parents included arguments that were similar to volleyball; each player volleying verbal insults that would hopefully outshine the last insult hurled. Sometimes we'd hear them argue as we played in the front yard. The arguing would continue until they finally decided to part ways. I believe I was four years old when my parents separated. Marrying young may have had something to do with their problems but it wasn't worth asking because I felt in my heart that they were better off apart. I was never a child torn by their decision to divorce or one that would lash out for attention. I just wanted my parents to be my parents regardless of whether or not they existed under the same roof. One result of the divorce was their decision to allow me to stay with my paternal grandparents whom were already partially raising me already. Unfortunately, this decision wasn't expressed to me and it cause repercussions for me later down the road.

I have very early memories of being raised by my paternal grandparents, Audrey and Odell, or Big Momma and Big Daddy as all of the grandkids so lovingly called them. They would care for me and my siblings when needed and always enjoyed having us around. Granted, I idolized and adored my grandparents but there is something interesting that happens when you feel as though your own parents abandoned you without cause. My mother tried to remain in Houston but after a short while she decided to return to Ville Platte, Louisiana where both of my parents were from originally. My younger brother, sister, and an unborn brother by a man other than my father at the time also relocated with her.

Life with my grandparents was a life that was filled with uncontested love and mutual adoration. They could honestly do no wrong and in my eyes because they were like Gods to me. My grandfather was a proud man who worked very hard to provide for his entire family and rarely ever complained. He was also a quiet man who often enjoyed an ice-cold twenty-four ounce can of beer, when they existed, as well as a glass of crown royal. I collected the purple Crown Royal bags and used them to store my loose change. I have very fond memories of him sitting in his recliner, drinking a can of beer, and partaking in a Houston Astros' baseball game. Sometimes, I'd sit with him just to be in his majestic presence although I couldn't care less about watching baseball. I just wanted to be in his presence. In him a saw a hero, a protector, and the man that I would eventually hope my own father would be for me. He was a man of a few words but when he spoke it was as if E.F. Hutton had entered the room; you listened.

My grandmother, who was also raising my two older cousins as well, showed all of us a great love that I still feel can never be replicated during my lifetime. Her word was final, but you didn't mind because you knew that she had your best interest at heart. She was an educated woman and was very proud of her family. She also supported us even when we did not deserve it. I still feel a little tingle in my soul when I attempt to remember her as the regal woman I found her to be. I remember the home we all shared as being peaceful, consistent and a safe haven for others who may have lost their way temporarily. I couldn't decide who was more authoritative because they wielded authority but just in different areas. They also loved and respected each other a great deal. My grandmother received whatever she wanted but she also made sure that my grandfather lacked for nothing as well. Overall, I did not lack for any parental love during that point of my life because I had what I considered to be two parents and two grandparents that I felt were really working to create a better life for me.

Also, my paternal aunt, Brenda, played a large role in my development as she was always there for me even when it seemed as though my parents were not. After my grandmother's death she stepped in and continued raising me as if I was her own child. She gave birth to her two sons at the ages of fifteen and sixteen. A few years later she required surgery that would render her unable to have more children. I often felt like the additional child she had always wanted. Some of my favorite moments in life were spent with her. She was one of my biggest cheerleaders. Admittedly, I was spoiled rotten and she knew it. I think she enjoyed it.

At the age of five my life as I knew it would take a drastic turn for the worse. My grandparents, cousins, aunt, and I took another one of our usual road trips to visit a great-uncle in my super-rural hometown of Ville Platte, Louisiana. At that young age my great uncle's home seemed majestic, endless, yet spooky when the night fell upon the walls. The hallway seemed to travel for miles but was rarely walked at night, at least not by me. One particular night, while lying in bed with a male cousin I began to feel a hand reach for the back of my underwear. I was lying on my stomach so his hand falling upon my body was shocking as I didn't see or feel it coming. A feeling of confusion set in along with a hint of fear as to what was going on. I clearly had no idea as to what was about to take place. A few minutes later I could feel a searing pain and realized that at that moment I was being raped. I had no idea what to call it at the time but I knew that it was wrong and that I wanted it to stop. I felt as though the pain and confusion muted my ability to scream yet I remember a lone tear falling to the pillow under me. It didn't last but for maybe a few moments and it may be due to the fact that penetrating me was too difficult for him. He hadn't whispered a single word before, during, or after the rape. That overwhelmingly powerful moment would become permanently seared into my mind and would forever change my life and how I viewed myself against other occupants of the world.

That painful and bewildering incident served as the beginning of what would be the dark years of periodic sexual abuse. That first experience left me feeling confused, shocked, alone, afraid, and disconnected from the world around me. I knew that what had just happened was not normal, yet, I had no idea what it was or who I could tell at the time because I felt a subconscious pressure to not say a word. There were no words spoken to me during the incident but I felt a loss of control and fear due to my cousin's size and stature. Everything and everyone is large to a five year old. I also knew that life as I knew it would be forever changed and definitely not for the better.

Over the course of almost seven years a total of four different men, including three family members, would come sexually violate me in some type of way. The type of violations I experienced at the hands of my perpetrators ranged from fondling to anal penetration. I can still remember the feelings of anxiety coupled with the intentional mental absence that I had to invoke in order to get through the occurrence of each assault. One of my violators, in particular, was much older and had authority over me at times. His son and I are cousins and were very close in our younger years. He only violated me once but it was enough to haunt me forever because of how "slick" he was that I could not notice what was going on until after it actually happened. At the age of nine or ten my younger brother and I were visiting our cousin. His dad was there watching over us. We thought nothing of this configuration because we had been there at other times prior to this without incident. I was the oldest child in the apartment and I was summoned into a separate part of the home. I can't remember exactly which part but I was definitely separated from my brother and cousin while they played as usual in the bedroom. My cousin's father was drinking something from a can but I was not sure exactly what it was. He asked me if I wanted some. So, like any curious kid I took a sip and remember the highly acidic and bitter taste of it. Before I knew I was being offered more and more while hearing his "friendly" tone of voice speaking to me. I eventually drank what was at least half a can. To a ten year old that had never had anything more alcoholic than Nyquil it felt as if I had drank two shots of Jamaican rum. The room began to spin a little and I knew that I needed to lay down in order to make it stop. My younger brother and cousin were still playing in the room; totally unaware of what was transpiring. I wasn't even sure what was transpiring. Moments later I was led to the master bedroom to "sleep it off". I was positioned on my back and I was prepared to sleep off the effects of the alcohol. But before I could fall fully asleep I would feel prying hands tugging against the back of my shorts. Then, I remember my shorts being pulled down to reveal my buttocks and two large hands rubbing that area of my body for several minutes until I eventually blacked out. When I awoke I was fully dressed but still slightly dizzy from the beer I had drank a couple of hours prior. I felt a sharp pain in my rear but I could not recall the reason why so, like prior incidents, I filed it away to never speak of it again. That was the lone violation I experienced at the hands of this person.

The series of violations that I feel were the most damaging were at the hands of whom I attached the title of "the family pedophile". I use this term to portray the damage that unsettled family secrets can have on a network of innocent people. But, I wouldn't even call this a secret because I had later come to find out that many people in my family knew of his behavior but chose not to adequately protect current and future victims from his actions. The revelation of this fact set the tone for years of resentment on my part because I know for a fact that I could have been spared the torment and degradation of my spirit had the proper action been taken at the right time.

I remember the time period it transpired because I was also in the seventh grade and it was one of my worst years in school for me. Not only was I being molested by the family pedophile I was also being bullied in school so my esteem was at an all-time low .The moments with him usually consisted of him separating me from the rest of the kids at night. No one thought anything out of the ordinary because most of us would bunk together since space was somewhat scarce. He was a master manipulator; a smooth talker of sorts who could talk his way out of a scheduled execution if necessary. I always knew what was about to go down. But, by this time I felt powerless and at some point believed that this was going to be my normal. There was absolutely nothing pleasurable about the experience. Like clockwork he would use some type of hair styling product as lubrication then grind against me until he ejaculated all over me. I had no idea at the time what it was. I just knew that once this happened I was going to be allowed to go to sleep to face the next day as if nothing ever happened. I still remember the weight of his body against me and his heavy breathing in my ear; becoming more rapid as his excitement grew. I remember my eyes being wide open and that we because he never faced me while he was abusing me and it almost always happened at night. Then, like a dirty dining room table I was wiped clean after being used and that was it until the next time. There were times whereby I was asked if I wanted to perform oral sex on him. I laid motionless and said not a single word hoping that my body language was enough of an answer, until he proceeded to place his penis in my mouth. I don't remember sucking but I remember his hips gyrating back and forth in enjoyment. I felt totally disgusted with the process and further disgusted with myself. I began to dread bedtime because I began to have nightmares that I was being taken away by some energy force. It was without a face but I knew that I had no power over it. I was once again overtaken and victimized. There was truly no rest for me.

The bullying and the molestation would happen throughout that year. Yet, no one at home knew of either happening to me. I was a small child and I was bullied by two larger girls who were obviously held back at least a couple of years. I was verbally berated while in class, at lunch break, and any other moment that they found an opportunity. I also remember being pushed and falling down a flight of stairs. The embarrassment and feeling of powerlessness as a result of the bullying was so overwhelming. As an eleven year old I was toting so much baggage that I am surprised that I never attempted suicide during that year because every single day was an intentional act to just exist. I don't remember having many of the carefree moments that young children usually have or should have. I was aware of everything around me; sounds, smells, faces, body movements of others, footsteps coming towards me, as well as any bump heard in the night. As a child I was exhausted and beaten. The feelings of heaviness, discomfort, fear, and uniqueness would lay the pavement for the outcomes I would experience at the hands of others as well as myself. The love of SELF left my building for what I felt was a permanent departure.

Years of not knowing what to properly call the sexual violation lent to my feeling of disarray. I absolutely knew it was wrong but what in the hell was I to call it? I felt that I had matured so quickly that unless I knew what to call it I couldn't possibly disclose it to anyone. So, it just lived within my soul as complete disarray. Also, the males in my family were rarely ever emotionally proactive. They were accustomed to reacting after the fact so I had no communication model to follow for a young man who had EVERYTHING on his heart to talk about. At the time I did not realize how large of an impact it had upon my stuttering problem. The reliance on my own voice would dissipate slowly over the years until I became virtually quiet. The self-hate grew like mold; eventually infecting any positive thought I may have had about myself. Dad

For years I would wonder why I was one of the targeted children in the family. I later learned that my family had a history of sexual abuse that was known but not neither treated nor reported. So, in the wake of incidents like these were other souls that were misguided, shaken apart, filled with self-doubt, and looking to the wrong things or wrong types of people for comfort or confirmation. Like them, I struggled with negative relationships, an unrealistic view of what my future could be like if I wasn't in this body, a negative view of my image as well as a negative perception of my value as a living human being.

While visiting my mother in Ville Platte, my grandmother had arrived from Houston to retrieve me to go back home. Upon her visit there she suffered a major stroke and within a short time she passed away. It was all so sudden. One night I was with my cousins playing while the older ladies in the family stepped out for awhile then next thing I know my life line, the only mother I really knew at that time, was gone. As a seven year old I was so confused because I knew my world had once again become undone but was uncertain of just how much so. The person that I relied on for comfort and confirmation was gone. Although she had no knowledge of my sexual abuse I felt that she knew I was confused and scared and always provided that comforting shoulder that I so desperately needed. I honestly felt as if I had nothing to look forward to. I remember being at the funeral and just being there. Confusion was present but I had no way to show it. Maybe it was my protective mechanisms at work but I sometimes wished I had allowed myself to grieve because without grieve there is no resolve to the feelings of being hurt, angry, and disappointed. Years later I still mourned her death because I realized that I never had a chance to say good-bye and I always wondered if she knew how much I loved, idolized, and adored her.

I don't remember crying or even talking her death much after it happened. I just remember our household back in Houston being taken over by a somewhat cold existence. I realized then that Big Momma was the glue of our family and without her we were all destined to become unraveled. To this day I don't think that most of our family ever recovered from her death. There was a dependence on her that was transferred to other things such as drugs, sex, and other unhealthy things that shook our family apart. When I mention family I am referring to my grandfather, my father, my aunt, her two older sons, and myself. These people became my rock and my shelter so when they fell apart I consequently followed but no one really knew. I imploded and began a long and slow downward spiral that would cause me to bottom out emotionally several times before realizing the amount of control I could have over my destiny.

My grandfather began to date other women. I was never jealous of the women because even as a child I knew that they had nothing to do with what had transpired in our family. I also wasn't upset that he was trying to be happy in his life. I was upset because I felt like I was not as important now that he had other people to focus his attention upon. For so long he had been my security blanket and the man that I looked up to. I never wanted to stand in the way and I had to understand that as he dated he had to give some of his attention to these women. As a result I felt abandoned and somewhat detached from anything that mattered. My father was around but I idolized my grandfather. If anyone would go to bat for me it would be him. No matter what, I thought the world of the quiet giant and I still do. My aunt was also a major force in my life. She took over the role of mother. Sometimes, I felt that she wanted me to believe that she was my mother as opposed to the mother who was alive and well in Louisiana. Anyway, she took great care of me and made sure that I was a priority.

At age twelve was when I remember having my last experience with sexual abuse. It was at the hands of another older male cousin and it started at least a year before. This time it happened more than once. When we'd have sleepovers with the other cousins he would always assign me to sleep with him even though he was several years older than me. I now believe that no one saw it as a problem because our homes were always short on space so we had to make do with the space we had. There was no penetration involved but the repercussions felt exactly the same. Everything about it was for his gratification. I was forced to masturbate him or allow him to lay behind me while he got his rocks off gyrating against me. I felt like a rag doll or an emotionless member of his dark world. Outside of that we virtually had nothing to talk about.

As I said before the molestation lasted for several months and by that time I felt so alone and very much a drifter that I didn't say anything. It wasn't because of fear but moreover because of the fact that I felt that I wasn't deserving of being heard. I conditioned myself to believe that this was going to be the formality of my life. Then, one day out of the blue I decided that I had had enough. It was mid-day on a weekend and I happened to be at my great aunt's house. I became sleepy so I decided to retire to the garage/bedroom for a nap. I began to feel that something was going to happen but I disregarded it as extreme paranoia. Like clockwork, he arrived in my bedroom, disrobed, and got in the bed with me. The moment I sensed his presence I jumped up and walked out of the home and walked the two miles back to my own home vowing that I would never go through that again. Luckily, I never had to experience that type of trauma again. But, the repercussions of the events would have a significantly negative impact on my life from then forward.

A few years before this time my natural father had become involved with a woman who had a daughter who was younger than me. Before becoming seriously involved with my future stepmother my father was very attentive to us even though he and my mother were not on good terms. I fondly remember him taking all three of us to his home and making us home cooked Cajun meals. I also remember feeling that my father and I were deeply connected. I was born a day before his birthday and I remember finding my baby book and seeing "he is my birthday gift" scribbled inside of it. I did not resemble him in any way but I did manage to inherit his small ears as well as his stutter. To me it was as if someone else knew my language and could understand how I felt when I stuttered. I wanted so much for him to be my hero but his relationship with his children took a drastic turn for the worse when he and my stepmother became one. We were no longer the priority and it became a bitter battle for his affection and attention. There is definitely some resentment that lingers from this but not nearly as much as there was several years ago. I had to learn that he is who he is and for me to spend valuable time in my life trying to rekindle something on my own is depriving me of valuable emotional time I could commit to my son, my partner, my friends, and the family members that I still have close ties.

I had gone to live with my mother at various times throughout my childhood and teenage years. It was myself and my three younger siblings and I can still remember how economically disadvantaged we were at times. I cringe at the use of the word "poor" because although we didn't always have what others consider an adequate amount of resources we did get by with a certain amount of love that would comfort us through most of our trials. At one point we only had two spoons and three forks so we had to take turns eating dinner. Also we had no plumbing that ran to the single toilet in the home. We also wore hand-me-downs and received donations from local churches during the holidays. In addition, we were on public assistance. My mother worked and tried her best but looking back on it now I realize that it takes so much time and energy to parent one child, let alone four. I will just say that these events have taught me how to be humbled by the simplest of amenities. Sometime later my mother became involved with my future stepfather. He was and still is a great provider and took care of my mother and four children that weren't his own and that alone made me admire him in a way that I had never admired another man. But, the problem was that my resentment toward my father prevented me from recognizing the great man that lives in my stepfather. I had not always resided with my mother so there were times of contention between what I knew growing up with my grandparents and my aunt and the harsh reality that I was now the big brother of other siblings that I had to take care of. Fortunately, through years of open dialog we were able to accept things as they happened and move on to build a wonderful and respectful relationship. My mother is far from perfect but she recognized that I needed answers, whether painful or not, in order to resolve my feelings of rejection of abandonment.

The side effects of my experiences with sexual abuse and rejection began to noticeably manifest themselves in middle school. Physical education was a required course and in most cases it was required for us to dress out which means that I had to wear shorts and t-shirt during class. I was so self-conscious of my body that I could not bring myself to disrobe in front of other guys and usually took a grade of D or F for failure to put on gym clothes because I was terrified of changing my clothes in front of other boys. I became intimidated by men because I did not trust them and I had no idea what to expect. I made friends with mostly girls because I felt that they had never let me down although I did yearn to have a "homeboy" to hang out with. I didn't mix with the usual guy cliques and sports were out of the question. I realized that I had begun to despise anything that dealt with being a man although I had no desire to be anything other than a man myself. I felt as though I was just here but not really identifying with anyone or anything. Also, moving around a lot after the death of my grandmother caused me to lose friends so much that I just stopped putting out the effort to make any. I stayed to myself and turned to my love of poetry, writing, and music to keep me company.

Throughout my childhood, my favorite cousin Darlene and I were as thick as thieves and we were always together whenever possible. I always felt a sense of understanding from her and we seemed to always complement each other's personality perfectly. Little did I know that we shared similar dark secrets. The same men that molested me were also the same men that molested her. One of the molesters, who happened to be her uncle, was caught in the act. He was scolded but nothing came of it because his habits grew worse and it was almost as if it was brushed under the table. This was one of the main reasons why I did not come forward as a child. If nothing came of him after he was caught then what reason would I have to come forward? He continued his reign of abuse on other family members as well as other young girls outside of the family. I became embarrassed, disgusted, and angry at the events that were seemingly ok to everyone else who witnessed it. Within those years I learned that sexual abuse goes far back into the family tree and that I had to first understand the root cause before I could understand the symptoms. I ultimately distanced myself from that part of the family. I felt that it was my only choice if I was to heal myself and save my own life.

  Then, there was the drug abuse that affected my life. My loving aunt had fallen victim to crack cocaine during my tenth grade year in high school. My family was accustomed to hearing about marijuana usage but this was on a different level. I heard the whispers from family members and noticed a change in both her demeanor and her emotional availability to me. The entire scenario of having a drug addict in the family was very foreign to us. Our family has its fair share of alcoholics and chain smokers but I believe this was our first up-close and personal brush with something that was so debilitating and so destructive and in such a short amount of time. I can recall the degradation of her mind and spirit as the evil of the drug took over. The aunt that could do no wrong in my eyes had become a shell of a woman that had grown dependent on something other than pure love. This was the first time that I felt that neither my love for her nor the love from the rest of her family was strong enough to undo what had already been done. For me, it was very difficult because our needs always came first with her and she worked hard to meet them even if she had to go without. She was just that caring and beautiful of a person. But, this time, it had nothing to do with me and there was absolutely nothing I could do to help her. We usually talked all the time about everything but I think she was sparing me from future devastation. Her addiction shook me to the core as I felt abandoned once again. I had to become my own parent of sorts. I was often seeing myself off to school not knowing if I would see her when I would return or what state of mind she may be in if I did. I would hear little things being said within the family but not many offering a hand of support. I now feel it was because everyone figured that if she wanted to stop using drugs then it was as simple as willing herself to do so, but it wasn't. I resented them for a long time for the way that they treated her because she had always been a very giving and loving woman even when it seemed she didn't have much to give. Even during her years of drug abuse she would still give of herself when she could. I considered some of my family a group of perpetual users who were only happy when their own needs were met. This is definitely an extreme view but my love for her was stronger than practically any other person in my family. I also felt a great deal of resentment towards myself because there was nothing I could do to help her.

I had learned that she had started to exchange sexual favors for drugs. All the while I knew in my heart that it was her addiction that was causing this behavior. She also started to befriend questionable people and I became internally irate. I cried several nights praying that God would save my "mom's" life. My once stellar grades in school became disappointingly low and I was on the verge of failing my sophomore year in high school which was something that no one in my family would have ever expected of. The breaking point was when my aunt asked me to go to a somewhat dangerous part of the neighborhood to purchase crack for her one night. I was upset but I had a hard time saying no to the woman that treated me as if I was born from her flesh. So, instead of lying I left the house for a while then returned saying that I couldn't find anyone. Now, we all know that if we wanted to find a dealer we could. I think she detected my hesitation and asked nothing further of me. It was at that moment that I decided that I would not be a contributor to her death and made the decision to finish my high school years in Louisiana with my real mother.

As usual, high school was the worst for me no matter if I was in Louisiana or Texas. Because I moved around a lot I had to end up making the same friends all over again as if I was the new guy in town. Side effects of my abuse and neglect began to show up at this time. My stuttering had grown worse and it only added to the surmounting pressure of everything else going on internally. I was labeled shy and quiet because I virtually stopped talking to anyone who did not know me. The years of being ridiculed by other kids and having people look at me as if I was retarded also bit deeply into my already sunken self-esteem. Also, there were moments when others would perceive me as being mentally ill only because I had a hard time saying certain words. I had gotten great grades in school so I was offended when people thought that my level of intelligence was subpar only because of my speech impediment. As a result, my insecurities were heightened. Now, I had to deal with the ramifications of being molested, the fear of abandonment, and the fact that I longed to have a normal voice just like everyone else. I tucked myself away in the shadows at every opportunity and was afraid of the unknown which made it that much more difficult to explore the fantasies that were held captive in my head. Those fantasies were actually my dreams of being successful and a complete person who was ok with who I was despite whatever existed within my physical body.

Mirrors and cameras felt like reflections of self-hatred as I tried my best to feel confident in my self-worth and self-image. I was told that I was attractive but it fell on deaf ears because I didn't feel that I could ever be attractive if I never saw myself that way. All the while no one in my family knew the true extent of my pain, self-torment, confusion, isolation, and my need for acceptance and confirmation. Inside I was hurt from so many things that I just prayed that I could get through each day with most of my sanity intact. I'd daydream in class about things such as having a different father, one day coming home to find my grandmother waiting for me, as well as having the strength to tell my family about the molestation. As long as these truths were buried within my soul I truly felt that no one knew well enough to ever love or help me.

One incident involving unprovoked violence that I had never revealed to my family happened at the age of fifteen. I remember it being a very pleasant and sunny spring day and I had decided to make the usual trek to my great aunt's home to spend time with my some two of my favorite cousins. Now, when I think about it, the walk had to be at least three miles and it would partly explain why I was so thin for many years. This day started out as any other weekend day. I happened upon the area of my former middle school. I was in tenth grade at the time so I really didn't think much about the school because I had no pleasant memories that I could recall. While walking along the sidewalk that bordered the fence of the school I noticed a group of young men who were obviously middle-school aged but seemed to be converging in a friendly manner. I was walking in the opposite direction of the group of young men but on the same sidewalk. Crossing paths with the group of young men was inevitable. I was raised to be hospitable so I thought nothing when I was shown the customary "what's up" head tilt from one of the young men. I said "what's up" and was extended a hand to shake. I was caught totally off guard when I began to feel blows to my head and face. What began as a nice spring day turned into a brief moment of violent torture at the hands of people whom I had never met nor intentionally provoked. I remember seeing at least eight young men at the time but had become paralyzed with fear. I do remember thinking, at least briefly, that this was the usual for me and that I was yet attacked again without reason. Luckily, an adult male was in his driveway and witnessed the beginning of the attack and broke it up. It may have lasted for maybe 1 minute and I walked away as if nothing happened. Little did I know that it would further my belief that I was destined for hurtful relationships and that there was nothing I could do about it. I was a random victim of street violence but I instantly concluded that it was just a part of continuing life story.

The saddest part is that I walked away expecting it again at some point in my life. This thought process made it easy for me to process and move forward although it was one of the most dangerous of thought processes that I could enlist.

Later, I arrived at my aunt's house and no one noticed anything peculiar or at least they never made a mention of anything being out of the ordinary. I was sore but I said nothing at all. Maybe I felt that no one would protect me anyway so why bother. I truly feel that my need to hide the occurrence was what aided in my body not revealing any major tell-tale signs of the assault. Another reason why I chose not to say anything at that time was because I was against violence from an early age and did not believe that hurting someone else in return was the way to heal my heart and my spirit. Setting soreness aside I decided that I was going to be fine. As crazy as it sounds I think I cared more for my perpetrators' safety rather than my own. I truly wanted to forget that it happened but realistically I couldn't. I did not want to be considered as a weakling or a failure to the "manhood" creed and that how I felt often times when I was around other males. I was often told about how men protect and stand their ground even if it meant that you would engage in violent behavior. But, I had a conscience and thought that I could never inflict on another human being the same pain that was inflicted upon me. Through it all I found that I genuinely loved people and knew that not all people were bad. I just had to get to the good ones so that they could change my current opinion about the bad ones.

High school graduation was interesting for me because while everyone was crying tears of joy and sadness about not seeing friends anymore I had no real high school friends and I was thinking of the next part my life's journey. I was so close to becoming an adult and part of me could not wait because I figured that being adult has to be better than what being a teenager turned out to be. Three days after my graduation I decided to move back to Texas. I had no real plan but I knew that I had to begin my life as an adult on my terms. I had nothing against living in Ville Platte at all. It was easy and predictable but I realized that living life the easy way and playing it safe served me no real purpose. I don't know what it was but I felt that I had to live outside of my normal environment in order to discover everything that life would have in store for me, both good and bad. I had yet to understand that I was in need of some emotional healing. My continued need for approval and acceptance would manifest itself through several bad relationships, lying in fear of being judged, severe depression, dangerously low self-image and an undying need to feel that I was truly a part of something special. Little did I know how much living it would take for me to understand myself, my demons, and my angels.

"My brother and sister, at this table you are invited to come as you are. You require no permission to be exactly what and who God designed you to be. Feast upon my kindness until your spirit is satisfied. My only job is to love you as I am commanded and to bring you closer to His presence by reflection and emulation of the same grace and mercy that is bestowed upon me and renewed daily."

[The application of God's definition of love as found in 1 Corinthians 13:4-8 ESV]

CHAPTER 2
ACCEPTING YOUR TRUTH:
LETTING THE SMOKE CLEAR

> **Personal Pledge:** I will learn to accept everything that has already happened in hopes of understanding why it may or may not continue to happen. My need to accept and forever present my truth will never be overshadowed by my need for acceptance and validation. As I sow the seeds of my truth I shall welcome a bounty of trust and authenticity that can neither be questioned nor dismissed.

Mostly everyone has heard the phrase "The first step in recovery is admitting that there is a problem." It is a part of human nature to hesitate at the sign of trouble because a decision must be made and that decision is usually to stand in defense or run. I fondly remember those moments where I felt that accepting my life as it was somehow meant that I was defining myself as being less than normal or substandard. I definitely wasn't close to accepting my entire truth because of fear that I would somehow be labeled as inadequate as compared to everyone else around me. I now understand that my delay in accepting the truth of every situation that bore weight upon my spirit was one of the costliest mistakes I could have ever made. As a result, I usually tell people that healing doesn't begin until you are ready to accept the complete truth of any problem. The truth can be a very ugly truth for some but we all have at least a little "ugly" hidden behind the curtains. It's just that some of us aren't afraid to wear the T-shirt that says "My truth is exactly what it is but it does not have to control my present steps".

When I speak of truth I am referring to everything involved in constructing the fabric of your being up to this point; including all positive and negative aspects. It ranges from the greatest moments of your life to your darkest hours. Wouldn't the process of evaluating your life feel more comforting if you were able to think of your life in its totality instead of focusing only on the negative events? The complete embrace of your entire story may allow you to recall more events of pleasure and happiness that can serve as a weapon against feelings of low self-worth and inadequacy.

To put it differently, finding your truth brings more substance to your reality. Each person's reality is shaped by their experiences, circumstances, environmental exposure, and the way each has been processed and handled. The handling of an experience refers to the decision that was made after the situation was processed. Did you decide to ignore it? Or instead, did you decide to face it head on at some point? There are a few other choices available but the bottom line is that each of these choices will somehow affect your perception of your reality. So, in some regard, you are able to answer your own questions as to why you perceive the world the way you do. How many times have you felt confused by your own perception of things? Part of you wants to believe what you feel but the remaining part of you has little self-trust therefore you are unable to truly enjoy most of life's joyous moments. The way you feel may not be valid for someone else but it is very valid for you and that is important when we attempt to learn to trust ourselves and our inner voice. The first indication of necessary change is when you feel the need to change your reality into something more positive and rewarding.

Coming to terms with the complete truth of your life can be a very frightening and tedious venture because it may result in the exposure of truths that are still either too painful and/or fresh to accept, were buried and forgotten as a means of coping, or are still too confusing to sort out. But the benefit of this possible upheaval is that it serves as a marker for where additional work is required. The commencement of this work may ultimately lead to a place of expanded peace of mind and emotional resolve. It also serves as an important benchmark that can be used to measure your emotional development and dexterity as you go through the healing process. It is extremely liberating when you are able to not only own your complete story but also tell it, if and when necessary, in a way that ends up being more beneficial for the listener as opposed to be more painful for the storyteller. But this peace and acceptance happens over time and may require an abundant amount of prayer, practice, and patience before it can be considered perfected.

I will be the first to say that while some of my truth was very catastrophic there were also moments that I consider jewels that helped to somewhat balance the chaos and noise. I can now say that my truth included loving grandparents, other people in my life that showed me love in great measures, sexual and physical abuse, feelings of neglect, low self-esteem, and confusion in regards to my reason for living. Notice that I acknowledged both the good and bad. This is important because we sometimes have to find the balance so that we do not become purposely focused on only the negative aspects of our lives. Balance provides us with an extension of positive value that we sometimes feel does not otherwise exist, especially during tumultuous moments in our lives. I learned the value in saying, "It is my truth and there is no requirement for anyone to believe it because I am secure in my truth."

About two years ago I had an acquaintance mention to me that the reason why he enjoyed speaking with me was because I was living in my truth. I had to ask him exactly what that meant because I didn't feel that any of our conversations were ever out of the ordinary or warranted any specific type of commendation. He told me that I spoke of my life effortlessly and that there was no hesitation as I shifted from speaking about great moments in my life to sharing the painful experiences. I had no idea that these actions could be labeled nor was I trying to invoke a deeper level of thinking. What I took from the compliment was that I was finally able to love and respect myself for all that I am and that included being a human being. I was also able to speak of my life without regretting the circumstances that I had no control over. I wasn't as far off as I used to think and I learned to celebrate the things that make me great and to work on those things that I feel deserve attention based on the goals I hope to achieve and the type of life I hope to live. The truth was that I was indeed a beautiful person. I just needed some fine tuning to bring forth my best qualities while attempting to repair years of pain and confusion.

As humans we are all prone to error but sometimes we forget to apply this principle when we evaluate ourselves. For some of us, failure on any level can spiral into self-hate, low self-image, and repeated self-condemnation which makes the ramifications of failure much more severe than expected.\. Sure, failure can be and is often hurtful but it is also an opportunity to discover areas of weakness that can be fortified if it is under our control. Also, it makes room for some of the most valuable life lessons after the grief process has passed. If we recover properly we also strengthen our spiritual armor and become more attuned with what it is that we need to sustain a certain level of stability and sanity. By accepting your truth you subconsciously allow yourself the freedom to explore remedies that are appropriate for your situation. That breath of fresh air becomes easier to ingest and process because no longer question whether or not indeed deserve it. Instead, you understand that like everyone else you deserve the best that this life has to offer.

I wanted to touch on religion for a brief moment because I truly feel that our religious and moral beliefs play a major part in how we either punish or celebrate ourselves and others, pattern our next steps, how we perceive ourselves against the rest of society, and our purpose here on earth. I remember, as a child, sitting in church with my mother and/or family on several occasions and hearing the preacher say something to the likes of "God makes no mistakes" and "Your life was planned long before you were born." I found it confusing for a long time because if my God made no mistakes then why did I feel as though my life was a series of mistakes that could only serve as something negative and shameful? Why was sexual abuse, neglect from my father, and my aunt's drug addiction part of my life plan? Also, what part of the plan included the death of my grandmother at such an early age? I wondered how these words could be spoken so confidently and how did they expect those words to resonate within me when I was filled with so much fear, anger, resentment, and self-doubt. . If I had no control then how could I possibly prevent the same things from happening again? It took several years for me to understand the importance of my spirituality and how my beliefs could positively reshape my identity.

I had grown accustomed to being afraid to speak about myself because my confidence was extremely low, but it was my way of life from a young age so I could not tell the difference between low or high self-esteem. It had become normal. My family assumed I was quiet because I had nothing to say but by not living in my truth I was also lying to everyone that mattered. Although I was too young at that time to practice the concept of living in my truth. I knew that the pain I concealed would ultimately come to hurt me in my near future. It was as if I suffered death to various parts of my being during different stages of my development.

It is true that life, for some, can resemble a long and arduous process filled with several rounds of reinvention and recalibration. Part of living in your truth is admitting your capabilities and limitations and not seeing them as faults but as unique attributes balanced by other stronger and more reliable attributes. For example, I've always had difficulty managing my finances. I am a college graduate with a master's degree in management but I still cannot balance a checkbook to save my own life. So, I had to come to a point where I had to admit that this was not one of my stronger attributes and that I would have to exude more effort to enhance my ability to complete this task. We will always find what seems to be a deficit to our character but we must ask ourselves if it is really a deficit as opposed to something that doesn't make or break who we are. You may not be the handiest person around the home but you may be a master in the kitchen. You may also not be the best person to list every detail of a project but you are great at getting the work done once the details are provided. What we see here is a stronger compliment in one area that makes up for other areas in which we may not be as strong.

Owning your complete truth also involves accepting your life as it comes as well as coming to terms with what has already passed. Things that have happened cannot be reversed but we can learn to control how that manifest as a result of future events. The fact that harm may have been inflicted upon you or you may have inflicted harm on someone else cannot be changed. This does not mean that you accept defeat. It simply means that you are able to open yourself up to discovering why particular things happened, especially if the events seem to happen in a habitual fashion. It is true that we sometimes purposely or unconsciously block out certain events in our past as a form of defense but what some of us do not realize is that the truth always comes out and mostly at inopportune times in our lives.

It was very difficult for me to accept the fact that I was sexually abused because this is something that I felt just could not have happened. Nor was it something that I felt I could ever reconcile. Growing up southern Baptist I remember hearing, quite a few times, in various sermons that men who lay with men were instantly sentenced to an afterlife spent in Hell. Yet, no provisions were made for actions that were done against one's will. So, I had no way of distinguishing between consensual sex and the blatant act of rape. The word ABUSE was so explosive to me because I felt I would be labeled without my consent, so I never spoke of it and acted like it never happened. This allowed me to seemingly live my life as every other person and not having to deal with the side effects of the events. But, I didn't realize until later that the patterns of my life were absolutely altered by the occurrences of abuse. By not living in my truth at that time I deprived myself of understanding what happened and accepting the fact that it was a part of my past. I also deprived myself of getting the help that I so desperately needed to heal and to live.

Many of us are afraid of confrontation on most levels. More specifically I am referring to the type of confrontation that involves facing our common worst enemy; ourselves. Self-confrontation can take on many forms but the underlying fact is that it is all about accepting things the way they are at this very moment. Some things may appear when they are actually chaotic and disconnected. In other words, one may have become disconnected with the painful realities as a form of a defense. The longer you believe nothing wrong is the longer you are putting off discovering what you need to be a successful human being. Without full acceptance of the terms of your current life you are depriving yourself of being emotionally available for the healing process. It is said that healing cannot begin until we acquire a full understanding of the problem or problems.

I had to confront myself on many levels and at different times in my life because certain problems were reoccurring because I had not faced the honest truth about them therefore increasing the probability that they may occur again; sometimes with a stronger vengeance than before. I persevered through the stages of feeling dumb, crazy, isolated, and alone because I could not stand the things that I was learning about myself. The dangerous relationships, the unusual ways of gaining acceptance, and the low regard I had for myself all had a common denominator which was ME. When we subtract the crazy boss, the abusive boyfriends, and the unsupportive friends, and the not-so-inspiring environments we are left with ourselves to deal with and that is when we are able to objectively look for root causes to our pain and confusion.

The process of self-confrontation is going to be painful for some because we usually aren't ready for the revelations that come to us as a result of the process. All the while we pointed the crooked finger at other people, places, or things for our problems and not really giving ourselves the opportunity to apply rationale to our solution processes. You may find yourself becoming emotionally drained at first and that's because you are forcing yourself to see yourself for what you really. The sometimes unrealistic view that you had of yourself may cease to exist and make you feel as though you are rediscovering yourself all over again, similar to the dating process.

At this moment I'd like you to think about some of your darkest moments in your life. Also, think about everything that contributed to that moment. Was it truly all your fault or were your actions merely symptoms of a deeply imbedded problem? Acting out or lack of action is usually a symptom of a bigger truth that we have yet to uncover. Why are you violent? Why do you tend to cry all of the time? Why do other people seem to take advantage of you? Why does your luck seem to never exist on the positive side of life? Why do you settle when you yearn for more? Why do you yearn for more when you know you don't deserve it? You deserve answers to these questions because they will serve as a backdrop to rediscovering who you are.

In the beginning it can be scary and difficult when you come to realize that you may not fully recognize the person you thought you were. But, at the end of the day it is a great thing because you are able to lose yourself (in a positive way) in a subject that has escaped you for many years and that is your own life. Who else is better equipped to answer questions about your life and your way of living as factually as possible? You are. The answers that come from yourself should not have to go through a process of trust and reliability, but again, this only happens when you are honest with yourself about yourself. Let me make it clear that this is by no means a method of getting answers to particular circumstances. Instead, this self-discovery serves as a way of knowing the far reaching effects of those circumstances.

Taking the time to get to know your TRUE self plays a large role in your overall confidence and self-esteem. Whatever was left to learn about your strengths and weaknesses will be uncovered. It's quite possible that you may come to realize that you were stronger and more equipped than you initially believed. Surprisingly enough, you will also find yourself becoming less offended when others recognize certain aspects of your truth and classify them as weaknesses. After all, it's hard to feel bad about something that you've already come to terms with. For example, why get upset if someone calls a procrastinator if deep down inside you know that it is absolutely true. Over time, you will begin to speak proudly of yourself and others will take notice of your sincerity and honesty and it will invoke a sense of mutual trust that you probably had never experienced before. That trust will enable you and others to see you for who you really are and you will find that your concern for judgment will decrease

Another benefit I've discovered by living in my truth is that it forced me to take inventory before I could really say that I respect who I am. It's extremely difficult to validate yourself by loving an image that is incorrect. I learned that whatever I try to hide about myself will eventually come to light and it's almost always at times when it is most unfortunate. Learning the importance of living in my own truth was a slow and sometimes painful process because at some point I relived the very events that created the most damaging moments of my life. If I was to be successful at this I had to force myself to accept that I had a role in my own detriment. I had to break my entire being into components that could be heavily critiqued either positively or negatively. I could then begin rebuild my faith in God, people as well as in myself by applying appropriate judgment and allowing myself to turn my mistakes and hardships into lessons for learning.

1998 was a very emotional year for me. I was near the end of a relationship that began very promising and enjoyable. Towards the end it became emotionally and physically abusive. I had my fair share of issues that I brought into the relationship but I would not discover exactly what they were until the very end. It felt as if every insecurity and shortcoming I possessed had somehow come forward during that relationship. My fear of abandonment was definitely there and I know this because I knew the relationship should have been over long before it officially ended, but I was not in an emotional position to let that person walk away from my life. Merely having them there was sometimes enough for me, whether their contribution was positive or negative. I viewed love as disaster recovery for my emotional turmoil. I also viewed that person as my super hero, someone sent to save my life. My expectations at that time were unrealistic and it proved to be too much of a role given to that person over my life. They took advantage of that role by expressing a sentiment to me that was destructive both to my mental state and my physical body. Yet, part of me knew that I had to carry some of the blame. That relationship forced me to begin to look at my life in reality. If I didn't understand why some people hurt me before I sure as hell figured it out at that time. I put out an energy that craved to be rescued, molded, and ultimately taken advantage of. The people that hurt me knew that it would be harder for me to leave them because they were, at times, my only real sense of belonging.

It was in that same year that I would master the art of self-pity and loathe my own existence. My significant other at the time had finally broken up with me for good. They had taken up with someone else but I refused to part ways. We lived in the same home while they pursued the new relationship, sometimes bringing the new boyfriend over to sleep in what used to be our room. Once again, my need to feel a part of something made me lower my dignity and self-respect to a level that allowed me to accept disrespect and to disrespect myself. The days that followed were filled with crying, sometimes without reason. I remember my eyes hurting and not knowing how to stop. I also remember not working and lying in bed for days on end without any motivation whatsoever. Slowly, I began to realize that I was doing exactly what I had always done. I put my self-validation in the hands of the person I loved. My value was based on their acceptance of me. When the smoke cleared I was an empty shell waiting for my next phase of validation. I finally had enough and I wanted the pain to stop.

Finally, I want to stress that your pain, dismay, disappointment, anxiousness, and happiness are all real. Sometimes, we are made to feel as though those emotions, whether appearing rational to others or not, are somehow unreal. It is true that members of the same family who live through the same experiences can have totally different viewpoints on the situation. Does that mean that either viewpoint is more important? Absolutely not. This fact is predicated by various elements such as the role of the family member (i.e. oldest child, youngest child, or parent) and how their view of reality has been shaped thus far based on related and unrelated circumstances. It would be very harmful to negate the pain or confusion that someone may feel merely because someone else doesn't understand it.

If you can feel it then it is real and cannot be considered invalid. By discounting the validity of those feelings may lead you to believe that the feelings, along with the associated events, somehow disappear. In reality it only delays the inevitable and it begins to drain your life as its energy source until one day you combust and possibly end up causing grave harm and danger to yourself and others around you. The truth is always available for discovery and is yours to own, stand in and live through. It only requires defense when you decide to do so but is almost always unnecessary. No one is required to acknowledge your truth but those that listen to you with their hearts will understand why it is important for them to accept your truth as a means of completely understanding who you are. By taking ownership of your complete truth you are taking the first step in the direction that is necessary to live in the present.

INTERMISSION I: The Mirror

Interpretations of reflections are highly subjective
Opinions of what is seen and felt can vary greatly depending on the viewer
Two people staring in the same mirror may envision something completely different
While one revels in their near-perfection the other may crumble at the sight of what they consider to be imperfect and quite possibly unacceptable
While one can smile and laugh at the stories that once made him cry
The other may deny that his presence on this earth is truly justified
While one takes the time to celebrate his uniqueness and can enjoy the beauty of others because of his own security
The other contemplates another lie that supports the last lie that masks the truth of his lack of self-acceptance
While one can stand in front of the mirror at any length of time without flinching
The other finds the mirror to be a painful reminder of the beauty that seemingly escaped him
While one lives boldly despite what he sees staring back at him
The other lives to spite everything that is before him
The reflection is always subjective and is at the mercy of the beholder
Sometimes it reflects the needs of the soul that yearns for repair
Or it may portray the perfectly imperfect person that always existed.

CHAPTER 3

DEPRESSION: THE DARKNESS THAT BLOCKED MY LIGHT

> ***Personal Pledge:*** *I will come to understand that emotions can be compared to light. Certain forms of light are meant to be brighter than others but when the order of brightness changes I owe it to myself to find the source of the disturbance. Ignoring the disturbance may lead to permanent darkness.*

I wondered whether or not to write about this topic but I had long decided before beginning this book that I would tackle all subjects as an adult speaking to other adults. In telling the story about my battle with depression is my hope to bring awareness to a disease that affects millions of people. If left untreated it can lead to severe consequences for the victim as well as others who may be directly connected such as family, friends, and associates. I felt the need to validate its existence and possibly bringing forth the realization that someone may personally identify with this story either personally or with the desire to help someone that they know and hopefully respond to the calling for the help that they may desperately need.

Have you ever been consumed by something at such a subtle pace that you didn't realize it had overcome you until it was too late? Depression is just that way. It is patient in its effort to take over your life and it usually succeeds because the victim had no idea what's going on. Depression can present itself as a dark, cold, seemingly endless, paralyzing, unrewarding, incapacitating, deafening, and bottomless moment in time that usually has multiple occurrences and can stretch over a large amount of time. Also, it is usually mistaken as a mood that is comparable to being sad. The problem with that comparison is that a mood is usually temporary and short term while depression can last for long periods of time and can be damaging both to yourself and others around you. That's why it is important to recognize depression for as a medical disorder. This is the only way to recognize the capacity for devastation associated with the disorder. Unfortunately, many believe that the terms "I am depressed" and "I suffer from depression" are synonymous but they actually aren't. So, do not be discouraged when friends and family members are quick to reply with "you'll be fine" or "just get over it". It may sometimes anger you but just know that it is their lack of understanding about the subject that makes them retort in that way. It may be up to you to enlighten them once you have an absolute understanding for yourself of what it is that you are dealing with.

I had heard about depression but I believed what most people believed that depression was just another mood or some type of temporary lapse in joy. I had no explanation for the years of emptiness I felt nor could I provide myself with a sane explanation of why I could not see what others saw in me. My experiences with sexual abuse, combined with feelings of neglect and the unsettled loss of my grandmother, paved the way for my future episodes of depression. This is why I firmly believe that my depression existed not only during my years as a young adult but as early as my adolescence. Reality was bleak and unstable and I found it difficult to balance pleasure and pain when even the simplest form of pain overshadowed any previous rewards of pleasure. It was interesting because I could have the best day but still feel as though the day was uneventful and unrewarding. It was as if I would flush away any joy my soul held unto at the end of the day and anticipated the darkness come the next morning.

The worst part about depression is that it robs one of valuable time and that there is no way to rewind one's thoughts or actions and undo any harm that was done in the interim. You are unable to function in your normal capacity and everything suffers including yourself, your loved ones, your career, and your relationships. Depression can also manifest itself in ways that are physical in nature. During my early twenties I remember experiencing long bouts of fatigue and mental exhaustion. I would lie in bed for hours unable to coax myself into getting out and nor was I interested in discovering what the world may have had to offer on certain days. I knew that I would become part of the living had I stepped foot out of the bed but I was afraid of the impending judgment, which was something I conjured up in my own head. I also hated mirrors. I resented the view that was staring back at me because I knew that so much work was needed and I figured if I ignored my image that I would somehow become ok with everything I represented.

I believe that my depression began in my early teens, probably right around the time my aunt was in the beginning stages of her drug addiction. I vividly remember seeing myself off to school, sitting in geometry class and basically staring out of the window for most of the entire class period. I would reminisce about the times that my aunt and I shared together and how my trust in her was unbreakable. Then, the bell would ring and back to my reality I went. I ended up doing the same thing in each class. I would daydream either about what used to be or what I wish was true. Then, I'd go back home and fall into the mode of being alone, sometimes crying without any apparent reason, and wondering about the easiest way to kill myself. Then, I'd think about everyone who supposedly loved me. I could not bear the thought of hurting anyone so I felt as though I was staying alive for them. I spent several years tormenting myself and would become virtually paralyzed in more crying spells, countless moments of questioning my next moves, being unable to break unprogressive routines, and a sense of complete hopelessness.

All of my relationships, both platonic and romantic, were deeply rooted in my need to please as well as my need to feel substantiated as a human being. I learned the hard way that these were the worst reasons to ever become involved in any type of relationship. Before I understood that I was just as deserving of happiness as those that I attempted to make happy I would suffer both physically and emotionally just for the sake of feeling attached. In the end I had to own my part in every equation especially when I knew that I allowed certain things to continue to happen way past the threshold that I believed I had set for myself. It would take years for me to learn that love, in the simplest context, is not painful, derogatory, nor shameful, and should not be feared. Also, love should be exuded first from me and shown by how I treat myself. This treatment will advise others of the way that I wish to be handled.

At the age of twenty-four I decided that it was time to find an answer to this perpetual darkness. At that point I would have settled for any answer that sounded remotely plausible. I had decided to make my first appointment to see a mental health professional. The feeling of embarrassment had dissipated and the denials of the issues were long gone. I figured that it would be ok to finally admit what I was feeling to someone who was trained to help me and who was otherwise unconnected to me. So, I made the appointment that was to occur in two weeks. That first visit was very interesting; I talked about myself for a little less than an hour. I was talking more than I ever thought I would. I spoke about my physical abuse, sexual abuse, fears of abandonment, recent relationship, and most of the other hardships I could remember. I had never verbally listed everything I felt so the process was more revealing than I had thought. I asked the doctor for anything to make "it" stop. "It" included crying uncontrollably, fear of losing loved ones, the loneliness, low self-esteem, feeling used and dirty…all of it. By the end of the conversation I was diagnosed as having bipolar disorder, whereby my mood would swing from extremely high (manic) to extremely low (depressed). I had no idea what it was but I walked out of there with a prescription for Zoloft. Somehow, I felt relieved that what I had been experiencing had been given a real title. No longer was I to think that I was sentenced to a life of just being sad and crying uncontrollably when I really had no reason to cry at the time. For once I wasn't made to feel hyper sensitive, unmanly, or otherwise abnormal. I also thought that this prescription would fix everything. Boy was I wrong.

My wish came true. I received a prescription, or what I regarded as my magic fix. I hurriedly made my way to the nearest pharmacist and waited anxiously and with bated breath as my prescription was being filled. You would have thought that I was on the verge of discovering a wonder drug. I went home as fast as I could and hurriedly swallowed the first pill. I don't even remember drinking any water. Surprisingly, nothing happened at first. I was distraught and angry because I needed to be fixed soon. Little did I know that it took up to two weeks for the drugs to show any sign of effectiveness. For two weeks I waited for a sign that something was happening. Then, it happened. I became emotionally numb. I felt as though my highs and lows had become indistinguishable and I no longer felt present in my own life. My once bubbly attitude and emotional connection to those I cared about was replaced with a solemn agreement that everything was just even keel. The drug did exactly what it was meant to do and that was to subdue my highs and lows. But, I had come to miss some of the highs and lows that provided some of the color to my dark days.

One day I realized that I was still continuing to rely heavily on external sources for my peace of mind. The acceptance from people was being replaced with a drug. The thoughts of my aunt's addiction kept flickering through my mind and it practically threw me into a tailspin of personal conflict. There was this residual fear of becoming some type of addict while I still felt the need for my issues to be pacified in a way that I could not do for myself. I noticed that the medication did somehow comfort me but I felt the dissipation of the emotions that I did enjoy exhibiting. I didn't want to become so docile that I could no longer get excited over the little things but it was happening in that manner.

Several months had passed before I decided to attempt to take more control over my mental health. Slowly but surely I started to realize that everyone and everything that was causing pain and discomfort in my life at that time were somehow my responsibility. I started looking at the patterns of my associations. Each association fed into at least one of my unrealistic needs. Then, I slowly started to realize that everything in my life had taken some control over some part of me. It was as if I had divided the pie into one hundred pieces and only about four or five of the pieces remained that I could claim as my own. I wanted my pie to be as whole as possible which meant I had to learn to take back the pieces that I had so easily given away before.

But, how was I able to do that if I needed what everyone and everything brought to my life at that time? I didn't think I was strong enough to muster up the courage to say one powerful word. That word was NO. I had to learn to say NO to friends, family, and situations that were damaging to my emotional bottom line. I mattered only as much as I told them I did so now it was time to demand the respect that I felt I deserved. It was by no means an easy road because I had spent so many years making sure that I pleased everyone as much as I can. Who was working for my pleasure? Sure, I had a handful of supportive people but the majority of the people did not know that I needed that mutual pleasure of feeling wanted and desired without having to do anything to earn it. I don't blame them at all. They were just working with what I gave them.

The day I came to this realization was the day I decided to stop taking the medication. I placed the bottle of medication in the back of my medicine drawer and told myself that I would not rely on medication until I took the initiative and searched for answers to my problem. From that point on I viewed medication as a last resort. At that moment I felt a sense of empowerment that I had not felt in years.

I do not discount the benefits of medication and psychiatric help at all. In fact, I urge you to investigate treatment options especially if you feel that your behavior can cause further harm to yourself or others. However, I do feel that sometimes we may look for immediate answers that pacify instead of attempting to take the time to discover why we are comfortable living in a world where more miserable than happy. At some point the story gets old and those around you are just waiting for you to discover what they've known about you for as long as they've known you. Factors such as family history and environmental conditions usually go overlooked if we are not taught to recognize their impact on our lives.

I convinced myself to depend on a drug to fix my problems before investigating less evasive solutions. I believe that did it backwards. I had yet to form the belief that I was strong enough to handle my own life. Could this be the very reason why my aunt had fallen victim to drug-abuse? Also, was I repeating the same acts that lead other family members and loved ones to turn to other sources of comfort that were both dangerous and addictive? I certainly thought so. I became frightened at the prospect of ending up distraught and hopeless while my problems persisted to get worse. I also became frightened that I would end up like my aunt. Witnessing the deterioration of such a loving spirit was the "scared stiff" moment I needed. I did not want to lose focus of the potential I had. The most valuable lessoned I learned in that moment is that I am all that I've yet to become. In that I mean that I recognized that there were deficiencies in my life that needed to be resolved. Also, the resolve of those deficiencies meant that I was bound to find success on another level that, at that time, was unfamiliar. But, I knew that it was to be.

Sometimes we find ourselves literally fighting within our minds. A part of us knows of our potential while another part of us replays the negative "what if" scenarios over and over again until we actually believe that our life is comprised of only those scenarios. If any of these prior statements sounds familiar to you then you owe it to yourself to take the steps necessary to get your life back. Unfortunately, most of us go as far as hitting rock bottom before we begin to understand that time for change had long arrived. We were just too afraid to follow it.

That dark place where I once took up residency was beginning to look very unattractive. I began to fold back the layers of my pain and confusion to find that almost all of it was rooted in my childhood and my inability to reveal and properly cope with the issues that had adversely affected my life, such as the death of my grandmother, the remarriage of my grandfather, my feelings of abandonment from both parents, sexual abuse, partner abuse, and my aunt's drug addiction and her subsequent death. No family is perfect by any means but I feel that at some point the dysfunction begins to feel normal which makes it harder for us to not become a victim of its poison. We have to learn to appreciate both the joyous and saddening moments and somehow find balance when creating the reality that we face every day.

The answer for you may include medical intervention or simply talking to a professional that can help create the bridge that is required to make positive changes towards healing and management of your depression. Some of you may find that medical assistance is necessary on a permanent basis. Whatever the proposed resolution, I urge you to become proactive in your own treatment and ask questions that will help you understand the root cause of your problems. From that you can learn how to recognize potential pitfalls and avoid them or learn how to work around them. There came a point in my life where I had to evict particular people from my life because their personalities served as a conduit to my confusion and dismay. Sure, some of them became bitter and upset but I had to learn that I am my own priority and I deserve to treat myself with the highest level of regard because people take notice as to how you treat yourself and usually treat you according to how you treat yourself.

Now is the time to make YOU the priority. Depression is a disease that desires to rob you of all that is bright and optimistic. It also attempts to consume your spirit and to force you to believe that your world is filled with despair and that you are not worthy of almost any type of sustained enjoyment. Make your first goal a simple one and attempt to be present in your own life. Begin to tell yourself everything that you wish you believed were true and that you are deserving of happiness. You may not find it to be true during this point in your life but there is great power in vocal expression. Often times I felt a sense of renewal when I was able to verbalize my thoughts and feelings. The same goes with journaling. I was able to hear and read my thoughts and over time it became clear that work was to be done in order to bring myself to a place of newfound courage and esteem. I had to make an effort to make this process as repetitive as possible. At some point I began to believe some of the great things that I had been telling myself and eventually you will too.

The smallest amount of success on your part should be applauded because it is a move in the right direction. It is to be understood that depression does not go away overnight. It is usually challenged on a daily basis and the more time we take to build our resilience the better we usually are. That resilience can also be found in sharing your struggles with someone whom you trust that will listen with their hearts and judge only when appropriate. You may come to find that there is a bond to be shared and you are no longer alone in the way that you feel. I encourage you to trust at least one person with your feelings and allow them the opportunity to influence you to see things in a more positive light or at least in a way that is different from what you believe your situation to be.

Moments of darkness pop up on occasion and I will probably always suffer from depression but I've learned to recognize the catalysts that invoke those moments while recognizing people and things that can help pull me back to the light. Being a father provides a new level of joy that always seems to provide the perfect medicine for those unbearable moments. I am shown true unconditional love that is pure and simple. I'm still in the process of learning how to find value in the simplest of things, such as seeing the break of a new dawn, watching my son grow into a young man, and allowing myself to take risks that are within reason.

CHAPTER 4
PAVING THE WAY FOR INNER PEACE

> *I want peace for my mind*
> *I want peace for my soul*
> *I need peace to make progress*
> *I need peace in order to accept that I am worthy of being loved*
> *I need peace in order to accept that I am capable of providing love*
> *I need peace in knowing that even when all is wrong it is still well*

The root to obtaining and maintaining my sanity was to first understand what drives me insane. By accepting my truth I had begun the process of accepting happiness as an element of daily living and not just an emotion that made its presence known on a few occasions. I had to shave off layers of anger, guilt, and depression to find the catalysts for such negative influences on my behavior and the way that I perceived my own value. But, how does sanity relate to serenity? Serenity can be viewed as that span of time whereby you exist in total peace and clarity. That peace comes from resolving events that you can control while understanding that certain things are not in your control, therefore letting it happen as it should. Clarity can come as a result of knowing yourself well enough to know when to "give in" to the fact that the situation is what it is. You are then able to make decisions with a less filtered point of view. This is where living in your truth comes into play. By accepting all of who you are you are preparing yourself to discover a new level of peace that will strengthen your self-confidence and provide a more consistent realm of enjoyment of life. So, it is safe to assume that once you are able to control your sanity (or insanity, for that matter) you are then able to graduate to serenity.

Serenity is also derived from acceptance of who we are and being ok with the reality in which we live. For example, I am African American, the oldest child of both of my parents and somewhat sensitive when it comes to how others perceive and respect my feelings. Most of the attributes I listed thus far won't change so it is wise for me to accept them as they are for that very reason. Once I am able to accept what is indeed fact I am then able to pattern my life's activities based around these facts. No longer will I create a false sense of who I am, especially if the facts do not support that vision. Also, the creation of a false perception means that I have to live up to that perception so that others can believe it. In essence, I would have to continue to lie about who I am and knowingly contribute to the lie as a daily habit. You will also find that others will easily accept your reality and witness your own level of serenity when you are able to own it. Most people can deal with things that they may consider to be a fault if the person who has the perceived fault is forthcoming and accepts it as part of their truth.

My stuttering had become a huge obstacle when communicating with people from as early as I can remember. As a child I was belittled constantly by other children and adults who had no understanding of the gravity of my disability. To them it was a joke that they would all join in on and would also soon forget as soon as the day would come to an end. But I saw it as a constant reminder of how "imperfect" I was; not yet understanding that we are all created with imperfections that lend to our uniqueness and authenticity. I felt I had no one to tell because my family had become so accustomed to my disability that to them it was rarely ever viewed as a hindrance. My "voice" was nonexistent therefore I felt I had no place amongst the bold and outspoken.

My inability to come to terms with my disability eventually affected both my personal and professional relationships including the relationship I had with myself. I worked so hard to vanquish my stuttering that my efforts eventually backfired therefore causing the problem to become more prominent. I'd freeze in panic when faced with situations that called for me to either read or speak aloud; especially in front of strangers. Anxiety would become my best friend for years. The mental torture I inflicted upon myself was usually worse than the actual act of stuttering. Couple that with my dealing with the ramifications of being periodically sexually abused I really felt that my voice, and my soul, was pushed further and further down the rafters to a point that I no longer believed that I had any truth left.

Eventually, I'd find comfort in both writing and music. These coping mechanisms would serve as my gateway to the outside world and as a way to express myself in ways that I felt I was never able to do before. I figured I was destined to be a silent communicator and continue to living a life that included allowing the voices of others to speak for or against me without remedy of any kind.

I never once considered simply managing it. I was so focused on denying it that it always came back to hurt me. I remember one winter day in 1998 I was on the phone talking to a prospective employer. I had a difficult time conveying my thoughts and became so disgusted that I hung up the phone right in the middle of the interview and cried. As I cried I began to once again fantasize about life in world where stuttering did not exist and where everyone could speak clearly and freely. I usually went there when I wanted to believe that everything was great in my world. But, this day would prove the most eventful of all days in the fight to become victorious over this situation. Shortly after my crying and self-pity episode wore off I received the call that I so desperately needed. One of my dear friends called and I explained my disgust with my stuttering. He simply replied, "You are the only one that makes such a big issue out of it." It was as if I had been revived from a conscious coma of sorts. I cared so much about the problem that it made others aware that a problem existed. So, I decided that I was not going to treat it as a problem but as an attribute, or a unique quality of my personality. It was as if someone gave me a stop-the-stuttering pill because from that day on I gained such control over my stuttering that it now became part of my sanity instead of what drove me insane. All I had to do was embrace it as a part of who I was. Once that was done I simply had to manage it just like every other part of me. I paid attention to what provoked my stuttering and found alternate solutions such as speaking slower, substituting words that I could not pronounce with words that had the same meaning but were easier to pronounce. I was taking control by learning to understand myself and my situation.

I was beginning to learn the concept of managing issues that were indeed manageable. Simply put, I learned that life is not to be spent trying to recover from trauma or to relieve every issue that plagues our lives. We should all, at some point, experience the joy in understanding that although our issues may have severely affected our current way of life we also have the capability of gaining more control of just how much of an effect they will continue to have. I learned that some of my best personality traits are directly attributed to some of my struggles and was part of a larger picture that made me a unique human being.

I continued to apply this concept of owning my issues and resolving them internally over the course of several years. I got the opportunity to know myself instead of waiting for that peace to come from acknowledgement from someone else. Let me reiterate that peace cannot come without understanding yourself to a point where you are ok with everything that you are. I slowly came to the understanding that God did not make any mistakes when He created me and I feel that this is the same for everyone. It's your charge to stand in your own light and come to terms with what your presence contributes to this world.

The only way to take a stand for yourself is to understand what you are defending.

Possession of a high level of self-appreciation and understanding can provoke a calmness and clarity that is required during one's journey of self-affirmation and improvement. This is due to the fact that we no longer compare ourselves unjustly but are able to use comparisons to find areas of improvement where improvement is available or warranted. Some things are meant to be just the way they are. As a parent I struggle with certain circumstances that my son faces and will face throughout his own journey through life. I wish to protect him at every pass but I realize that some things will have to happen in order to strengthen their armor as they progress in a world that may be harsher than the world I live in today. Although, I would like to foresee every event that takes place in their lives I know that a great deal of those events will be out of my control. The same thing applies to your life as well. You can only foresee so much until you realize that you are wandering blindly while attempting to reach that next destination. One of the most important things to do is to progress through your life as positively as is to work positively so that the unexpected events occur less often.

Now, let's speak in terms of conflict. In most cases we find that we cannot come to a peaceful resolution with conflict until we understand what provoked the conflict. The same is for serenity. Serenity comes as a result of finally understanding that what has come to pass is either resolvable either by finding the answer, confronting the sources of the problem or simply deciding that it's ok not to continue to seek the answer. One of the end results is that we learn how to control how often certain events occur, if ever again. These events I speak of can include financial concerns, issues related to maintaining relationships and personal growth. For years I had a hard time progressing because I spent an unusual amount of time during my day reflecting on things that had already transpired. I was a victim of sexual abuse at a very young age so as a result I was always prone to bouts of depression, low self-esteem, and fear of men in general. How does one find peace with this situation? Like forgiveness, we assume that being at peace has something to do with letting things slide without confrontation and acknowledgement. I'm sorry to inform you that that isn't the purpose of peace. The purpose of peace is to promote harmony either with yourself or with others whom you have a relationship. That harmony cannot exist while focusing valuable energy on circumstances and events that really do not matter in the grand scheme of things. At the end of the day you have to be accountable for your own actions, whether positive or negative.

During my early twenties I finally came to accept the fact that I was sexually abused. For years I downplayed my low self-esteem, fear of intimacy and abandonment, and lack of trust as the growing pains of becoming a teenager and never linked these attributes to my sexual abuse. But, these problems continued well into my late twenties and it became an exhaustive thought process, in that I had to convince myself daily that I was ok because the negative side of the situation had taken up permanent residence within me. The self-affirmation had to take a backseat until I was allowed a moment of freedom to actively admit the situation, think about how it affected my life, and devise a game plan to move forward in the right direction. Coming to terms with what had happened meant that I had to travel as far back as I could remember in order to see the picture for as large as it really was. I once again began to wonder why I was chosen out of all of the other children in the family. I had to come to terms with the fact that I could either ask my perpetrators why I was one of the chosen and mentally prepare myself for answers that I may not really want to hear or just understand that it is what it is without further endangering my mental well-being. Then, I had to look at my life to see where this situation could have a positive effect from this point forward. Over time I realized that my compassion for others, especially children, had been heightened by these events. The joy that comes from helping others triumph may not be as prevalent as it is now had it not been for what I had gone through. Increased empathy is and end result that I am so happy to have gained. So, I learned that whatever happened has made me into who I am today. Some of us do not get this far because we are still searching for answers that we do not need, therefore causing our own unsettlement. As a result we find it hard to come to any level of serenity. We have more control over our lives than we usually exert. The level of dependence on external forces to contribute positively to our lives varies from one person to another. We need those external forces but we can control the influence that they have on our happiness.

Living in constant unsettlement can be self-destructive and a deterrent to success. We become prone to achieving milestones in fragments instead of feeling a true sense of accomplishment that comes from completing an entire task. We may begin a new task with a heightened anxiety but find ourselves thrown off-track with isolated thoughts of despair. You never stick around long enough to read the conclusion of the story. The same thing happens to life without peace and serenity. We condition ourselves to not stick around for the finale of our own show because we're afraid that the ending would be too much of a cliffhanger to withstand. It is actually interesting for us to think that way without realizing that we had a large contribution to the ending of the story. So, in order to feel secure in your story you must make positive contributions to the storyline that controls the narrative flow of your life.

Most of us have heard of or read the Serenity Prayer, attributed to Reinhold Niebuhr, shown below:

> *God grant me the serenity*
> *To accept the things I cannot change;*
> *The courage to change the things I can;*
> *And the wisdom to know the difference*

I had read that particular poem several times before in the past but I never found a personal attachment to it until I made the connection that some of life's best lessons comes from questions left unanswered. Was it really that simple? Could I just tell myself that it happened, it was out of my control, and that I don't need the answers? At first I thought not. But, I thought I'd try it over time just to say that I gave it a shot. What more could I lose, right? Well, the challenge wasn't easy? I had to reassure myself throughout each day that I no longer had to ask myself why I had to believe that I can live outside of my circumstances. I really didn't need to know why. When I felt myself going into that zone I sometimes went to a mirror and looked at myself for seconds at a time while telling myself, "I had no control over what happened but I can control how it controls me from today into forever."

I had to make my serenity a priority and the actions that contributed to my serenity had to go from manually invoked to automatic actions. When I had major disagreements with people I learned to not wonder what goes on in their minds because, again, I cannot control their thoughts. I could, however, learn to somewhat control how people perceived me by carefully observing my own actions and determining if I was contributing to my own negative image. If so, I had to learn to own the behavior as my own, then decide if changing the behavior would contribute to the ultimate goal of where I want to be in life. I had to take care of my own mental health and become a bit selfish towards my own mental health. I was in no position to help anyone else while I was in such disarray. After a long drawn out battle with myself...I won. I became free to concentrate that wasted on energy on my current goals and aspirations. It became easier to deal with various circumstances that continue to happen as part of a normal life. I would usually shut down around very strong and opinionated people and become extremely intimidated because of my fear of people finding out that I wasn't as strong and together as I had been portraying. I was afraid to show that I was human and that I had imperfections as I am sure they did as well. I was afraid to just be happy with me. That was before I found my serenity. That was also before I made myself believe that not all questions were to be answered. I also faced the realization that maybe I wasn't ready for all of the answers I had been seeking.

We have to be careful to not overextend our search for answers. Sometimes, the answers are more painful than the question so we have to really be aware of how much additional pressure we place in our minds and our spirits. If the answers do not have an adversely positive effect on your life are they really worth seeking? Are you capable of telling yourself that you can continue to live a successful life in spite of the unanswered questions? Sure you are. The key is finding balance for what you desire and what you truly need. Maybe God has answered your prayers for clarity by not providing an answer because He knows that the clarity is not necessary for you to fulfill your destinies in life. He has purposely placed these circumstances before you in order to help you understand that you are stronger than what you perceive and that your enemies are only as strong as you allow them to be.

There are definitely circumstances where knowing the answers is highly beneficial. For example, if you are terminated from a job you would like to know the reason so that it can possibly help you keep the next job you get. Now, let's say that a close friend betrays you in ways that you feel are incomprehensible and you approach that friend to ask why he or she did what she did. Unfortunately, for you, the answer you receive only makes the problem worse from your point of view. Do you continue to ask questions in hopes of finding an answer that is justifiable to you? If you plan to possibly continue the friendship then I feel that it is without question that you resolve the issue. If your plans are not to continue the friendship then how much energy are you wasting on trying to find answers? Sometimes it's ok to just let things be.

Having serenity in your life includes the ability to convince yourself that it is ok just to know that everything happens for a reason. Sometimes, we come to realize those reasons days, months, or years after the event happens but we have to act in the now to keep serenity a constant in our lives. That means learning to be patient until the answers that we need are revealed. Notice I said "need" and not "want". Once we learn which answers are necessary for us to proceed with a successful life we will then be able to mentally release the desires for unnecessary answers that occupy essential time and space within our thought process. Then, we can repurpose that space by dedicating more energy on the topics that truly deserve our attention. Instead of wasting time on pointless things such as wondering why the road is curved instead of straight it would be better if you were to invest that time in pondering your next great move in your life.

I'm an avid believer that sometimes we have to document our thoughts in a way that allows us to review ourselves for sanity and validity. As a result of my depression I usually have racing thoughts that compete for sole attention so my thought process sometimes includes jotting down ideas or questions and reading them back to myself. Then, I perform what I have termed "self-check". I use the term self-check to refer to the process of rationalizing one's thoughts before being expressed or acted upon. Some of the thoughts or ideas I have pondered may have seemed totally logical within the confines of my own mind but later proved irrational and unattainable once I wrote them down or said them aloud. For example, I once considered studying to become a physician's assistant. But, I had to realize that I really don't care to see anyone else's injuries but my own. It was a great thought but I soon realized that I really had no interest in what some of the work may entail. Isn't it better to learn the art of self-check as opposed to being told by others, more often than not, that your thoughts are not rational? This level of self-awareness also lends itself to your level of peace. In order to be successful at this level you have to understand your own limitations and be able to apply your full knowledge of self properly and appropriately.

How many mornings have you looked out the window just before leaving work only to notice that the weather is not to your liking? Do you sometimes look in the mirror and hate the outfit you decided to wear? Have you ever attempted to start your car only to realize that your battery is dead? Do you sometimes question why your boss is seemingly rude at times? All of these questions are common for most of us but sometimes the line is blurred between what we can and cannot control. You can change your clothes but you can't change the weather. You can dye your hair a different color if you so choose to but you cannot change your heritage. Circumstances that can be changed sometimes require a plan of action while some only require a slight alteration in how you do things. When we have no idea what we can and can't change we sit and complain about it all. This causes us to become stifled in our efforts to change and our personal growth is severely stunted. We also become sorrowful and sometimes pitiful in our efforts to elevate our consciousness to understand that we can't control everything but we can control a majority of the things that dictate our desired quality of life.

Over time you will able to more quickly resolve your thoughts and ideas and become an expert at knowing yourself, your threshold for pain, and your ability to understand when an issue can simply be ignored. Then, you will discover a clarity that will allow those great thoughts to come forth more rapidly. At some point the great thoughts will overshadow the gray thoughts and you will understand the joy of serenity.

"Sometimes the most negative thoughts that influence one's current movement in life can be found in every past situation that has yet to be forgiven. At some point a decision must be made whether or not to accept the facts of what happened, remove invalid self-blame and forgive the entire trespass. It is at that moment that LETTING IT GO *has come to be and that* MOVING FORWARD *has begun."*

CHAPTER 5

THE POWER & FREEDOM OF FORGIVENESS

> **Personal Pledge:** *I will allow myself the opportunity to be free of the burdens that I am not meant to carry. Also, I will remind myself that forgiveness is my Godly right and that God shall forgive me just as I forgive others.*

This chapter of the book fills me with great excitement because of my eagerness to share my journey associated with forgiveness. Learning truth about forgiveness and harnessing its power is so transformational and I feel that its addition to your arsenal of personal empowerment tools can only enhance your quality of life. Forgiveness can sometimes prove to be the most exhaustive part of the emotional healing process because it usually involves the rehashing of painful events so that you can come to terms with what really "was" and how what "was" has been negatively influencing "what is". Some events in our life can bring tremendous joy while others may render us emotionally scarred on different levels. Sometimes we condition ourselves to those types of long-term injuries and learn to live life in a very sheltered and somewhat paranoid way because of it. This same scarring can permeate through generations as it leaves remnants upon everything we encounter. We can break free from the chains created as a result of pain, suffering, and confusion by learning how to reoccupy our thoughts with hope, confidence, and assurance that "what was" doesn't always have to be "what will always be".

By not practicing forgiveness we tend to pile issue upon issue and pain upon pain. I compare the damage to what happens to a balloon that is being filled with water ever so slowly. Balloons have a limited capacity. Every grudge that you carry can be symbolized as water, filling the balloon so much at each pass. Pretty soon the balloon begins to stretch severely out of place because of the work that has to take place in order for it to stretch and encompass the additional burdens (weight) that is placed on it by your grudges. The same happens to your heart and your attitude. You are forced to revisit your burdens and seemingly relive past events in an effort to keep them alive. Each cycle of this behavior adds pressure, or water, to your emotional balloon; incrementally expanding it. At some point there is no more room for expansion and your balloon has become completely filled. Once the balloon has reached its capacity it may either start to slowly tear or just burst completely. All of the water that was contained in the balloon now has the power to damage everything in its path which includes your spirit as well as everything and everyone that you have been or will become attached to. The emotional flooding has no mercy on anything in its path and it strikes without warning. The damage can range from mild to catastrophic depending on how many and the type of grudges you've carried. Ask yourself, would you rather have an occasional refreshing and cleansing shower or emotionally violent hurricanes that intensify with each passage?

Being unable to forgive can also be compared to self-torture in a sense that it is self-inflicted and self-controlled. Just as it is a choice to forgive it is also a blatant choice to not forgive. Failure to forgive can foster a type of anger resentment, or fear that others usually can't understand. For some, it can serve as the precursor to rage which is an uncontrollable and dangerous response to anger. As a result your response can come off as being irrational when compared to others who presented with a situation that is reminiscent of a prior event that still lives harmfully within your soul. The truth is that your expression of anger, resentment, or fear is only a symptom of the underlying issues. How many times have you been in a romantic relationship only to find that your insecurity about something that happened years ago with someone completely different rears its ugly head at the most inopportune time? You even try to rationalize it to the person that is the recipient of that insecurity. You already know that they are thinking, "Why doesn't he/she just get over it?" You find yourself becoming more upset when the person is unable to sympathize with you. So, instead of coming to terms with your issue you break off the relationship and attribute it to him; perhaps flying into a fit of irrational anger. Worst yet is when you decide to remain a victim of the adversity and hope that others will grant you an emotional pardon until you are able to get a grip over what it is that is haunting what could be a beautiful and loving spirit.

One of the most dangerous mistakes one can make as it relates to understanding the power of and navigating the process of forgiveness is confusing FORGIVENESS with FORGETTING. A vast number of people believe that the act of forgiving someone or a particular circumstance is somehow a request to forget every part of the violation that occurred. That couldn't be further from the truth. Forgiveness is to be viewed as a relief for the pressure of things that have already transpired and an agreement with yourself to gain more control over the quality of life that you desire but has been controlled and heavily marred by your past. I use the word pressure to describe the feelings associated with resentment and anger because of how it affects us when we DECIDE to hold on to it. It's similar to a swelling from the inside that is uncontrollable and unpredictable; sometimes resulting in reactions that can sometimes surprise us. Some of us choose to lash out verbally or physically towards others and sometimes towards ourselves. Or, we choose to, forego a brand new situation out of fear of what "may" happen according to your past. Finally, forgiveness can also block one's desire to take new chances in life that are absolutely required in order to advance to the next. The dismay associated with impending failure, hurt, or harm cripples the psyche; the typical example of failure to launch.

Some of us decide not to love again because of the pain we experienced prior without realizing that love was never the culprit. Yet, we hold love responsible before we come to understand that God's definition of love has absolutely nothing to do with our negative experiences and everything to do with the basic reason that we were all designed in his image; that is to dispense love according to His plan.

It is my strong opinion that one's emotional maturity is severely stunted when one is unable to forgive. Absent in the inability to harness the power and freedom of forgiveness is the emotional freedom that allows one to interpret specific life events more rationally and welcome the lessons that require permission to be received and applied. For example, when a situation occurs that evokes those emotions that we have yet to abandon or rationalize you will find yourself reverting to that point in time when the violation occurred and possibly reacting similarly to the way you did before. As a result, we most often tend to avoid similar situations or tip-toe around anything that remotely resembles those issues. We're afraid that if we forgive then we are giving someone the signal that what they did to us was ok; that we somehow agreed to the outcome. We are also afraid that if we forgive then it is a sign of some form of weakness and that we are giving someone the green light to hurt us again. We owe it to ourselves to attempt to come to terms with what has transpired and cause us such grief and confusion and the only way that can happen is if we approach it in as realistic manner as possible. The commitment to understand forgiveness gives us that opportunity to begin accepting a situation as it really is; an event that has occurred in a point and time that cannot be erased.

As previously mentioned forgiveness should be viewed as a right and a gift to yourself because you are allowing yourself the privilege of peace of mind and renewed clarity. This newfound clarity will have a profoundly positive impact on certain decisions you make from here on. I define forgiveness as the dissolution of resentment for what has transpired. You are indeed ready to let it go. You are also ready to stop the cycle of finding and placing blame for what has occurred. Also, you are ready to dispel the anxiety and curiosity of knowing why certain things happened. Finally, you are ready to break the emotional link to the person or persons that played a part in the event that caused you pain. All of this sounds great but I want to let you know that forgiveness is not a process that comes easy the first time. It is a reiterative process that gets a little easier each time. This by no means suggests that you will come to a point where you will forgive any and everything as soon as it happens. The grieving process is real and must happen but the grudge should not continue to cripple your progress.

I previously mentioned the benefit of peace of mind and mental clarity as it relates to forgiveness but there are other great benefits associated with forgiveness. For example, you will begin to have more meaningful and fulfilling relationships with others and this is because not only is your judgment enhanced but you will begin to see people more as human beings. This realization comes with the expectation that they will, at times, commit errors whether intentional or not. This has to be one of the most important benefits and can make the difference in the expectations you place on others. You will find yourself less dependent on others to make up for what someone else may have done to you. For example, a lover will no longer be held to task for an emotional or physical transgression committed by an ex-lover. This is only one example but the bottom line is that you will be able to create more nurturing and enriching relationships as well as being as nurturing and enriching to those with whom you choose to connect.

With a newfound ability to trust you will find that you are now able to accept advice that will lead to a better mental and spiritual well-being. Think about it, sometimes you may repeatedly question God by asking, "Why me?" and this is because you have yet to form the understanding that sometimes pain and loss can result in the best learning opportunities. The lessons are more readily available for us when we are able to forgive. The grudge itself prevents us from wanting to learn anything because we find it hard to believe that anything good can be born from anything so life-altering and chaotic. Yet, we may quite possibly be setting ourselves up to be hurt over and over again as a result. This is because we have not accepted that sometimes the hurt that was inflicted upon us may be directly linked to a choice that was willingly made. It's an awful reality to face when you have to accept that a chaotic event may have been rooted in a choice that we made from the onset. When we live as a victim we usually have no desire to learn. All we desire to do is continue to place blame and wait for comfort. Notice, I said wait. Forgiveness also empowers you with the ability to learn how to grant yourself the comfort you require from yourself without requiring the comfort of those that may have trespassed against you. You will also notice your ability to live more in the present because less thought and energy is reserved for reliving the past. Most times we can't see the future because we do not intentionally dedicate enough time to forecast and plan our next moves.

I'd also like to touch on some of positive the health benefits of forgiveness. Most of us have visited a doctor at least once in our lives for some type of illness or injury. One of the most common suggestions when recovering from an illness, surgery, or other medical event is to decrease our level of stress because our bodies react negatively to stress. A grudge is like cancer on an emotional level. It grows and sustains itself until it completely takes over your spirit. Although its formation is intentional it becomes so easy to accept that it because somewhat automatic. Then, it begins to influence every other opinion about any situation that is remotely similar to the one that sponsored the grudge. Holding grudges results in higher stress levels and the reason is that in order for us to hold on to the grudge we have to remind ourselves of the events that transpired thereby replaying the pain and dismay over and over again. It is that same pain and dismay that clouds our ability to always think clearly and rationally and it is that very confusion that is at the root of our stress associated with grudges. Not to mention that everyday life presents its own fair amount of stress so we owe it to ourselves to try to decrease it. Your life could be at stake.

    Most who know me would say that I appear to be very healthy. I assumed the same thing myself until I felt my world around me literally going white. It was mid-December of 2008. I was prepared to leave that evening to drive to Hampton, Virginia for training associated with a special project that I had to lead at work. The morning went by as usual outside of me making final plans for my trip. I was finalizing my hotel reservations and was planning to leave work earlier than usual so that I could forego getting stuck in as much traffic as possible. Around 12:30 PM that day I started feeling very weird. I am usually working on my computer so I figured that I may just need to rest my eyes for a minute so I turned to talk to one of my teammates who happened to be Caucasian. While looking at him I noticed that I could not see his whole face. It was as if I had been staring at light bulbs for about a minute. I saw large white globes of light where his eyes and nose should be. Then, all of a sudden I started having increased tunnel vision. It was as if someone had put white blinders over my eyes. I could only see in front of me because my side view had been totally eliminated. I knew something was wrong.

    I decided to visit the health unit at my workplace. Deep down inside I knew what it was but was afraid to say it. I arrived at the health unit and signed in. I told the receptionist my symptoms and sat down. About three minutes later a nurse called me back into the observation room. She tested my blood pressure and had this strange look. She told me to wait for two minutes and left the room. She came back to test it again and had the same look over her face. She then asked me for my supervisor's phone extension. I told her but she failed to tell me why she asked for it. She then told me that I should leave right now and check into a hospital. I became frantic. She then told me that according to my blood pressure that I could very well have a stroke at any minute. Next, I was told to take what I had and go directly to the hospital. She called my supervisor right then and told him the situation. I walked less than a block to the subway and started on my journey to George Washington University Hospital.

    Once I arrived at the hospital I checked in to the emergency room. I was seen almost immediately and was whisked into a room where I was told to take off my shirt and lay back in this large chair. The nurse attached several pads on my torso in order to perform an echocardiogram which basically takes a picture of the heart. I was then told that there were noticeable striations on my heart. I had no idea what all of this meant so my question to them was "Am I dying?" Instantly, I began to think about my son, Tyler and how his life would be turned upside down if I was to suddenly become unable to take care of him. I began to miss his smile and laughter almost immediately. I said to myself, "I'm not finished here, my baby needs me." It was such a painful moment for me that I cried for about five minutes because I felt as though this was a cruel joke after I had worked so hard to become better for myself. Luckily, I was going to be ok but I had to learn how to take care of myself now that I was diagnosed as having high blood pressure. I was thirty- five years old and diagnosed with stage 2 hypertension. This didn't feel fair to me at all but I had to deal with the truth. The first thing the doctor asked me was if I had been under extreme levels of stress for some time. This is why I can attest to how valuable stress management is to your overall well-being and why practicing forgiveness should become a standard part of your stress management plan.

I nearly died before I realized its complete value. I don't want this to be your story. It could be worse. Your final story could include death.

For years I could not get over my anger and resentment in regards to being sexually abused. I was no longer haunted by the fact that it happened but I was so focused on the fact that my perpetrators were walking around and living their lives without being held accountable for their actions. The pain transformed into sheer resentment and I wanted very much to hurt them in some way to make them pay for the years I felt I wasted feeling less than normal and used as a result of their indiscretions. I hated having to visit particular people in my family because at least one or all of my perpetrators would more than likely be present as well. I ended up distancing myself from my entire family and I felt as if I was the only one who paid dearly for that action. I had yet to share what was troubling me and a part of me did not want to interrupt the fabric of my family and hold blame for causing further conflict. I was sometimes considered the family member that thought he was too good to be around others but the truth was that I could no longer stand to be around people I felt harmed my life. I also separated myself because I felt no sense of protection. My safety net was nonexistent.

The hatred and disgust over the situation had built up over several years as my mind and body behaved in "victim mode". I often imploded and began hurting myself mentally by harboring these feelings. I felt that no one could understand my confusion and that my life was regulated to only suffer at the hands of others because I was conditioned to believe so. Some days I felt old and used while others days left me feeling exhausted and subpar. I was afraid to forgive because I was afraid to try something that I did not trust. And everyone I ever loved ended up paying for it, either in small and unnoticeable ways or through heated arguments that were usually one-sided and focused on me as the victim. I felt that holding on to the anger was a means of preventing the incident from happening again but in reality, I couldn't have been further from the truth. I was robbing myself of a clearer conscious and was afraid to live openly and honestly. I was living as a victim and unable to cope or make progress within my life. I didn't trust my faith and the belief that forgiveness, as an act with no physical attributes, is for the betterment of the practitioner.

    The inability to forgive is comparable to a dark pit that expands over time. It slowly engulfs our personal space and requires constant mental labor to exist. One of the other reasons why forgiveness can be so difficult is because we actually fear the end result. What does forgiveness look like? How will it show up in our lives? Do I trust myself enough to take that chance? The darkness sometimes takes on a life of its own that we cannot control. The "whys" invaded my thoughts so often that they became my primary focus. I had to try to live between going back and forth between my past, my present, and what looked like a doomed future. I often imploded when I became extremely aggravated when thinking about certain events of my life. I took it out on myself primarily while others around may have caught the tail end of my anger. I even became angry at the thought that the people who hurt me were not even thinking about me and how my life has been affected. Sometimes, we also assume that we can avoid dealing with pain so long as we have something to replace it with. For example, the loss of my grandmother could not be replaced by the presence of my mother. Although I love my mother dearly I had to understand that she was not my grandmother. In order to respect my mother's place in my life I had to also respect that my grandmother held a unique and irreplaceable position in my life. It wasn't until then that I was able to love my mother for simply being my mother instead of rejecting her because she was not my grandmother.

    Frankly, it came to a point where I felt I was on the brink of a nervous breakdown and I had to find a way out of my gloom and a way to escape from the part of myself that was stifling my progress as a human being. I found that escape by slowly coming to terms with what forgiveness really was. It was an extreme test of my faith in trusting the unknown. It still proves to be one of the hardest things that I've ever had to do but as I stated before, forgiveness saved my life. One day I decided to take inventory of all my blessings that I was able to enjoy in the present tense. I had come a long way from the shell of the person I thought I was; I lived in a nice home that I worked hard to obtain, I was highly educated, I was doing well in my career and I was blessed with the wonderful task of being a father to a caring and loving son. So, it was obvious that I had experienced great personal growth and that my past experiences were no longer affecting my current or future success as much as it did in the past. It was evident that the act of forgiveness was allowing me the ability to think much further along than I had ever imagined because I was no longer allowing such a great deal of my mental capacity to go towards events that I either had no control over or could not change at this point. The bottom line was that over time I was able to either let it go or learn to manage how it affected my life. As simple as it sounds that is exactly what happened.

During this same time period I recognized that my compassion for others had grown exponentially as a direct result of my adversities. I also felt as though my desire to be committed and present in my own child's life was shaped by the emotional absence of my own father. I was able to continue the act of forgiveness because all I could realize was positive results. I owned the process and I was learning to wield its power. I was not required to call anyone and say "I forgave you". It also did not require the acknowledgement or acceptance from the people that I forgave.

My capacity for forgiveness was once-again tested while visiting my hometown in Louisiana during funeral services that were held in the fall of 2008 for my dearly departed aunt. I traveled with my son from Maryland to Louisiana where the home going services were to be held. Family members who have not seen one another in several years were reunited and I have to admit that it was a very nostalgic time for me because I had avoided going home for over eight years but I felt this was the perfect time to return. The services were very touching and people, including myself, publicly recounted just how much her life meant to us and how her forgiving spirit still moves within us. I had not planned to speak at all but I felt moved to say a few kind words that turned into my testimony of how her love and adoration for me was one of the things that kept me above ground. After the funeral services were over most of the family adjourned to a local church cafeteria where dinner was being served. I was seated next to a cousin of mine and carrying on a well-deserved walk down memory lane. I didn't realize that sitting across from me was one of the family members that molested me. I suddenly realized that I had not one bit of anger towards the person. I still had no reason to hold a lengthy conversation but I did not feel the after-effects that I usually felt after being in the same room with one of my perpetrators. Forgiveness worked and I had proof. So, now there was no reason not to continue the practice.

Deciding what to forgive is also a process that may cause painful memories to resurface but I feel it is necessary to understand just what it is you are forgiving. Are you forgiving the person or the event? Sometimes it's one or the other or both. By forgiving a person we are releasing that person's hold on our subconscious mind. We are no longer concerned whether or not the person is thinking about what they did or if they are even remorseful. Also, we are also not concerned as to whether or not the person even wants to be forgiven. Our goal is to regain control over our own reactions and manage the effects that the situation may have upon our emotional standing. It also helps to restore trust in your ability to become a better judge of character as well as the ability to approach life with more optimism and less pessimism.

I had finally decided that it was time to set myself free because I no longer wanted to allow "them" to win at the game called "my life". The day I began to forgive was the day that I began to breathe lighter, think deeper, and live a little bit more carefree instead of living carelessly and too closely guarded. I cannot even describe the weight that was lifted off of my heart. My newfound belief in karma was a big contributor to my ability to forgive. I feel that we eventually receive the energy that we put out. So, I was sure that my perpetrators have been dealt with in ways that I could not explain nor care to explain. I know that I didn't want to allow anyone else to claim a victory over the success or failure of my life. I was finally able to speak about particular incidents without reverting back to a childlike state. Also, I could use my stories as scenic backdrops that could be used to empower others as well as to forge a sense of togetherness when most victims of any type of abuse feel alone and isolated.

One of the most important areas of forgiveness that escaped me for years was the forgiveness that was owed to my aunt who had fallen victim to drug abuse. I never blamed her for her drug abuse but I blamed her for taking away someone else that I relied upon. After my grandmother passed and my grandfather's remarriage she was the only person I trusted to love me without condition and to accept me as I was; the little boy who was stuck inside himself. She believed me when I spoke of my abuse and my feelings of detachment with my father. She also encouraged me more than anyone I can remember. To have that taken away by the infiltration of drugs was devastating to me. I felt that she let me down and that she did not love me enough to make a choice between me and the habit. Also, her fall from grace forced me to grow up quicker than I ever wanted to. I became a child and adult dueling within myself for the right balance. I protected myself while yearning to feel safe enough to let others in. I attempted to make my own way in life while hoping for someone wise to show me how not to make the many mistakes that I was bound to make. Her ascension into her drug habit left me hungry for attention and security. Years would pass before I would be able to understand just how much this event had changed my perception of the world and those that occupied it.

After living in Washington, DC for over two years I decided to take my first trip back home to Houston, Texas. I remember seeing my aunt and the first time we reconnected she flashed a smile that I had grown to love but had not seen in years. I was so happy to see her but afraid to attach myself out of fear of disappointment. I knew that she was still an addict but I looked into her eyes and saw a glimmer of the woman that she used to be to and for me. During our conversation she told me that she was always proud of me and that she talked about me and my accomplishments to everyone. It was in that moment that I realized that her addiction had not taken away her love and adoration of me and that her problem had nothing at all to do with me. I felt her shame for being an addict. I finally understood that as of that point it was not her choice to be an addict and that her body needed the drug to feel normal. It would take several years before she would become drug free but I began evaluate the problem for what it was. It forced to me to perform research and to help her as much as I could while being encouraging and unwavering in my desire to see her become healthy. We had several tear-filled conversations that she may have viewed as very strong and negative but I think she understood that I needed clarity and for her to understand that I was not going to be the family member that bad mouthed her. Yet, I was going to converse with her openly and honestly about my feelings and the effects of her habit while encouraging her with great memories of our relationship. I was finally able to forgive her and move forward with rebuilding our relationship.

The day came when she was able to acknowledge the impact that her drug abuse had not only on my life but everyone who loved her. I cried that day because for the first time I felt that not only I had experienced the power of forgiveness but that she had also began to forgive herself, thus jointly creating an environment that was highly conducive to healing and moving forward. Unfortunately, the living angel that had blessed my life so tremendously left this earthly dwelling in the fall of 2008. I am so happy that I had the opportunity to forgive her situation because I would have had to bear the guilt of not doing it sooner rather than later.

Ironically, while everyone was crying during the funeral and wake I was content in knowing that she no longer had to suffer. Her health was failing and I no longer wanted to see my angel in pain. They told me that she had gone into the hospital because she wasn't feeling well and that her heart just stopped. My spirit told me that she was simply ready to go. She had made peace with her life and decided it was simply time to let go and start a new journey. She is still the absolute most amazing woman that ever graced my life and I there was no way to be angry with God because she gave me what I needed with neither her nor I knowing that I actually needed it.

The process of determining if anything positive has come from your adversities is confusing because part of you will refuse to think that anything positive could come from everything that has hurt you. That thought could not be further from the truth. If that is the case then it is important that we learn to move into a space of peace and serenity in knowing that what has happened has affected you in a negative way but now you have the opportunity to find the light at the end of the tunnel. From here on you can learn to channel that anger and disappointment into living abundantly by recognizing that the best revenge for turmoil and strife is success and upward mobility.

Living a strong and determined life helps to deter disappointments because you will then be able to view each situation on its own merit, decide how much of the end result was controllable, and process each is event as rationally as possible by determining which actions play a detrimental part in your positive development. Think of how we usually reference a dark cloud to symbolize disappointment or strife. What usually happens to a cloud that has become darkened and heavy with water? It eventually dispenses itself unto the earth, releasing all that caused it to become overly saturated. During the release process the cloud slowly whitens and becomes less and less heavy until it is able to become indistinguishable from the rest of the clouds in the sky. This is how we should view our own lives. We are soluble creatures that absorb conditions of our environment, the actions and results of people who affect our lives advertently and inadvertently, and other elements that contribute to our lives either positively or negatively. Over time, our mental filters will want to hold on to more negative energy than we hope, thus slowly causing our mental cloud to go from a happy white space to a darkening grey matter. It is at that point that we determine just how much of this negative energy we will retain before we begin to release it from our being.

A subcomponent of forgiveness that seems, at least for most of the people I know, the most difficult to implement is the act of self-forgiveness. I can testify to the difficulty that one is presented with when attempting to adopt the notion that it is okay to set yourself free of bindings presented by a past that has left you feeling unaccomplished. If you are getting uncomfortable while reading this then it applies to you and could quite possibly save you from years of redundant blame.

A few months ago I was in the midst of what I call a "life-excavating" conversation with one of my dearest friends via telephone. We were discussing a relationship that he had recently begun but then I sensed that there was more to the story than he was willing to tell me at the time. His initial concern was whether or not he should move forward and take the relationship to another level. I sensed some uncertainty on his ability to make a wise decision so I asked about the source of the uncertainty. Sure enough, we ended up deep diving into prior decisions that he felt were disastrous or otherwise reaped negative consequences. Yet, I felt there was more to this conversation than just a fear of making a decision. Eventually, he revealed that he felt as though he had let down himself along with those that expected a different outcome for his life than he was currently experiencing. He graduated high school then immediately entered college as expected. Unfortunately, he only completed two and a half years. He dropped out of college and began his life as a workingman. Then, almost every important decision afterwards seemed to not go quite as expected. He continued to berate himself for at least another five minutes before becoming quiet as if he was awaiting some life-changing detailed response from me, which at times I was known to give. This time my reply was simple and to the point. "When are you going to let yourself off the hook?"

My question was greeted with a pause. I posed a question that forced him to think of the negative effects related to his inability to forgive himself for mistakes made prior or for the goals that remained unaccomplished. He was experiencing what we all experience when continue the cycle of self-blame, and sometimes self-condemnation, for what we feel our life picture should look like at a given moment. While in the midst of this anguish it becomes difficult to take into account all of the wonderful things we have either been blessed with or accumulated through faith, hard work, and perseverance. The end result is a wonderful list of blessings that have been muddied by a few major hiccups. The balance that has always existed between positive and negative situations must be restored so that we are able to continue to grow from our experiences, while still being able to rejoice in the milestones that happen along the way.

Throughout our upbringing we are sometimes forcibly imparted with expectations placed upon us by our parents, caregivers, and others that have a direct influence on our self-image and esteem. Also, environmental and situational factors play a noticeable part in what we feel we must accomplish or who we should become in order to either balance a life that we may feel was less forgiving, or to continue a life that we consider to be fair. For example, if a person was reared in an impoverished environment then it wouldn't be uncommon for the parents of that individual to try to influence their child, through obvious and subliminal messages, to strive to accomplish goals that would remove them from their current standard of living. This goal may not take into consideration what the child actually wants for his/her own life, but it exists because the parent wishes a better life for their child. The immediate issue with this practice is that it further invalidates a child's dream of what he/she envisions for his/her own life. Their passions, and quite possibly their purpose, usually becomes muffled under the noise of stress, influence, and the pressure of being directed to follow a path that they will later discover had nothing to with what they wanted for themselves. The inner child that is fearless, imaginative, and risky can easily become diluted, restricted, and lost in the shuffle of the world.

Letting yourself off the hook gives you permission to, at some point, wipe the slate clean and opens the door for learning the root of why certain decisions were made and are continuing to be made that are leading to incomplete goals and missed opportunities. It also alleviates the pressure placed upon one's spirit by expectations that took into little account that when events happen that are out of one's control it isn't always easy to recover and move forward as originally planned. In other words "life just happens" and we are forced to either roll with the punches or get sucker punched. For example, I can't attend college unless I am somehow able to pay for it, either with my own funds or with some type of assistance. Also, I can't get married unless there is someone else on the other end that I feel is equally yoked. If conditions in one's life change unexpectedly it is usually difficult for us to recalibrate and regain a steady standing. The ground becomes shakier than usual and this action becomes a hotbed for doubt, insecurity, and instability. In addition it also becomes more difficult to come to terms with the fact that either the initial goal has to be altered based on the resources available or scrapped altogether because further attempts to achieve it will result in failure and more disappointment. There are many more examples that illustrate the fact that we have to gain more control of what we can control (input from self) while accepting what we can't control (input and results from external entities) and adjusting accordingly instead of tormenting ourselves with regret.

One of the hardest things to admit and accept is that LIFE (including every occurrence controlled or uncontrolled) happens at the rate of less than a blink of the eye and sometimes the results just aren't good. In fact, it came downright devastating at times. A mere stitch in someone else's reality may adversely affect your reality and that is the moment when control is seemingly lost. It is also the time that one must yield to that lack of control instead of constantly resisting, often proving to be exhausting and painful. It's a harsh reality to deal with at times because we desire so much control without realizing that the very things we hope to gain control over will never grant us permission to do so. But, we can learn to accept and adapt to change therefore becoming more welcoming to the changes required to continue a more fulfilling life. There is absolute power to be gained when we are able to understand what is ours to control. Also, there is accountability to be gained when we know exactly what it is that we contribute to every equation. If we want to change a typical outcome it may be as simple as slightly altering what is usually done.

Let's take a moment and speak about the trespasses that we have committed against others. I have not met, nor believe, that there is one single person that has not hurt someone else, either advertently or inadvertently. This would include you as well. We have spoken words or committed actions against someone or a group of people that we may come to question years later because we have become better for ourselves and more intelligent to situations through education and edification. Compassion, empathy, and sympathy for the same person or people that were hurt by our actions may have increased because we've learned to take steps toward accountability and remediation. Apologies, whether spoken or written, were rendered as a sincere gesture of remorse. The bottom line is that we have all been in this seat probably more than once. The problem comes when we victimize ourselves repeatedly for a mistake that may have happened only once. The self-forgiveness you require only requires you and God. It's time to make peace with yourself as you've done with others and free yourself from repeated punishment.

As you well know, people hurt people for different reasons. Some of us hurt out of fear of being the first to be hurt as our past has dictated. Others may hurt others simply because they honestly do not know better or have never seen a positive example from which to pattern their response to adverse emotions such as pain, anger, sadness, and even confusion. No matter the case, there is a major reason why self-forgiveness is required. It increases one's capacity for self-accountability, and it allows one to dissect their behavior and discover the true root of their action. If an apology is in order then bestow it if possible. But, retain the focus of self-forgiveness because it lessens the chance for the occurrence to repeat itself and you will find that you are more liable to try to correct the behavior by enacting changes that will affect your levels of compassion, accountability, and sympathy for others.

Forgiveness of yourself and others should be regarded as an obligation to yourself for the betterment of your mental and physical well-being. It's the forever-valid hall pass that allows you to safely wander down the hallways of your life, visiting each room for a self-imposed period of time. Once the visit is concluded, you can safely close the door behind you while retaining only what is required for you to safely venture into the next room. Your backpack will consist of lessons learned that weigh far less than the regret and self-hate that you placed upon yourself and carried daily. Also, buried within your backpack is the higher prospect of better experiences with others because your expectations will not be born from the need for them to correct a past that they had no part in. Instead, the expectations will be born from how you expect to be treated because you were first able to treat yourself the same way.

All of these wonderful changes can and will most likely happen as the practice of forgiveness is enlisted. As previously mentioned you will not come to master it overnight but it will become easier and more fulfilling with each pass. As a result you will reap the following benefits:

- ✓ You will learn to set time limits on the grieving process for each event
- ✓ You will learn to evaluate each event for what it truly is and conclude what is needed for you to move forward.
- ✓ You will be open to lessons learned and new "life best practices" that will decrease the probability of the occurrence happening again.
- ✓ You will reconcile what is either controllable (your actions and contributions toward specific events) and what is uncontrollable (other people, places and things)
- ✓ You will ask yourself "how is my quality of life currently being affected by not forgiving and how my quality of life will improve if I do forgive?"
- ✓ You will move forward much quicker with less fear and apprehension.

If it is discovered that forgiveness is too difficult for you to enact on your own then it may be necessary to enlist professional help in order to reach that goal. I will reiterate that forgiveness isn't always easy to implement but it is it is a required component to healing. You have the opportunity to bring positive value into your current quality of life. As previously stated you need no one's permission. But, you do need to fully understand that forgiveness has nothing to do with weakness but everything to do with your inherit superpower. When you begin to smile in the face of adversity it diminishes its supposed control. At some point you will master the power of forgiveness and when it is time to do so you will understand that each step along the way allows you to catch up with the life that has continued to move forward without you. Your future can then be seen beyond the trees and forest and your aspirations will increase in scope because your thoughts will live more on the side of optimism.

"At birth we are destined for greatness. It is life's circumstances that sometimes deter us from recognizing our maximum potential"

Intermission II – The Runner

New city; same luggage; extended suffering
Never unpacking yet constantly expanding; eventually causing spillover
Hurt, anger, self-loathing, and premature emancipation were the initial results
It all took a toll on the man that never felt the joy of simply being a carefree boy
Worry, fear, abandonment, and neglect stunted my emotional maturity
It was their choice to either violate me or leave me behind yet I bore all of the guilt, shame and blame
Baby of the family in one household while struggling to lead in another; maximum confusion
Peaked and deflated repeatedly without a safety net to soften the fall
Each fall prolonged my recovery until I settled on being permanently emotionally disabled
Loving others more than I loved myself was my practice but definitely not the way to survive
The need for validation was like handing over the knife and granting permission to cut me deeply; simply to hear "I choose you" or "you are worthy"
Yet, I would again bear all the guilt and blame
Even to the point of begging for the abuse; all for sake of inclusion and attachment
Like clockwork, when fear and pain would couple against me I'd run again
But not quite able to outrun the truth that I was afraid to face
The truth was that I'd run in hopes of arriving to a new place
But I'd end up right where I began; stuck with myself
Stuck with dilapidated dreams, an injured soul, and a search for truth
The truth was always in my possession yet highly unrecognizable
Everything that was good was muddied by all things dark and misunderstood
Everything righteous became uncertain and fearful
While everything that was dreaded became my partner
I welcomed pain and confusion because I trusted and understood what was to come
Yet, I pushed away family because I had no clue of what the next moment would bring
Neither a lover nor a friend had the power to save me
Neither another lie nor another instance of ignoring my truth could spare me

So, I'd run further with a heavier load and an extensive burden
Still anticipating a moment that I could stop and unpack
Then, I began to replay Proverbs 3:5 in my mind
"Trust in the LORD with all your heart
and lean not on your own understanding;"
I began to understand that MY understanding/intuition/gut feeling was tainted by everything that was ugly and bruised
In turn, my reality was skewed and that it was time submit my heart and mind to a power that was greater than I could ever be.
In that submission I found peace, hope, and help
PEACE of mind knowing that my burdens were not always mine to carry
HOPE that the waters that once destroyed my shoreline would soon recede
HELP from a powerful source that would lead me to a place of independence
It was then that I decided to unzip my luggage; inspect the contents, decide what I should keep and what was not mine to carry, forgive myself for extending my own pain, forgive those that trespassed against me, await and accept the lessons that were awaiting me, and share those lessons with you
Hoping to help another runner reach the finish line

"The eye cannot say to the hand, "I have no need of you," nor again the head to the feet, "I have no need of you." On the contrary, the parts of the body that seem to be weaker are indispensable, and on those parts of the body that we think less honorable we bestow the greater honor, and our unpresentable parts are treated with greater modesty, which our more presentable parts do not require. But God has so composed the body, giving greater honor to the part that lacked it, that there may be no division in the body, but that the members may have the same care for one another. If one member suffers, all suffer together; if one member is honored, all rejoice together."

(1 Corinthians 12:21-26 ESV)

CHAPTER 6

IMPERFECTION: GOD'S PERFECT FINGERPRINT

> **Personal Pledge**: *God made not one single mistake in my design. I am flawed by design yet perfectly crafted for what it is that I am fashioned to do. I will recognize the surplus that has been gained by my deficit.*

Imagine a world where everything was picture perfect; not a hair out of place or a stone left unturned or unaccounted for. Also, imagine that every tree that you happened upon bore the same amount of fruit and foliage as the one next. Also, imagine if everything you had ever desired was in arms reach and that every perceived physical, mental, and emotional imperfection had somehow been corrected or never existed. Hold that thought for just a moment. Notice that I stated that the imperfection is perceived, which means that there is a reconciliation that needs to happen before some of us become comfortable with the fact that our imperfections should be considered unique character traits. Those same unique character traits set us apart as individuals and can at times provide some utility that benefits us. Sometimes the norm is the imperfection.

Is the light bulb glowing yet? If not then it surely will later on. How do you define an imperfection? Is it something that looks or feels abnormal or otherwise measures below what someone else considers to be a baseline for what is good or noteworthy? Someone deaf would more than likely consider their inability to hear as an imperfection, just as someone with a noticeable limp may classify themselves as imperfect. Even behaviors that are a result of certain circumstances may be considered as imperfections. Those are fair assessments but they aren't always necessarily true assessments. I want you to think about why imperfections exist. Some of us ride the negative train of thought and assume that imperfections are some type of cruel joke that God plays on us in order to "keep us in check".

While I do believe that acknowledging one's imperfections has a significant impact on one's level of humility, it is also my feeling that these acknowledgements can serve as motivation to unlock potential that must be utilized to provide balance for any perceived deficiency. We become much better equipped when we are able to acknowledge and accept our imperfections because it allows God the perfect opportunity to reveal to us the other areas in which we can perform greatly. Sometimes, the enhancements in other areas may already exist, but because we sometimes sit in despair as it relates to what we cannot do, we bypass those functions and attributes that make us masters in other aspects of our lives, as well as the lives of others we encounter. You are rarely ever handed a deficiency in your life without being blessed with an enhancement in efficiency in one or more areas. Simply put, if you truly believe that God makes no mistakes, then why believe that he all of a sudden had an "oops" moment when he created you in his likeness? (Insert LIGHT BULB FLASH here)

Imperfections exist for and are perceived differently depending on who you feel you were meant to be and the personal expectations by which you abide. Unfortunately, we all are not capable of interpreting imperfections in a positive manner therefore removing ourselves from a level of self-discovery that is critically important to our overall emotional development. It is my opinion that everyone accepts that they possess imperfections. What matters is how each person interprets and adjusts their life (goals, aspirations, and daily living) to accommodate the imperfection(s). For some, the imperfections may force one to utilize other resources more than usual to accommodate for a specific shortage. But, others may instantly create their own glass ceiling of achievement.

For years, I stood at a standstill, as it related to my stuttering problem. It was as if I would literally lose my breath at the thought of speaking publicly or being made out to be some type of "less-than-deserving" individual only because I could not enjoy the luxury of speaking clearly without being teased to the point of crying. As a child, other kids teased me profusely, and I remember, often times purposely being the quiet kid even if I had the answers that someone else was seeking. Everything I felt about my stuttering was what I assumed everyone else felt. I spent years projecting a negative image and expected it to come back just as harsh.

For years I felt that there was a problem with the fact that my family and those close to me never tried to correct the issue. I was never told by my family what I could not do as it related to my speech so I felt as if I skated through because they expected me to stutter. I also felt that they allowed me to continually make a fool of myself and wanted me to feel negatively about my self-image. I couldn't have been more incorrect. Even after correcting my stuttering issue I noticed that they had not said a word about the "new voice". Part of me felt the need for their acknowledgement over this victory. I was left disappointed when no such acknowledgement came. Then, one day I came to the realization that the reason why they had not said anything was because they had become more accepting of my disability than I ever was. If I had never corrected my speech impediment it would not have changed the way the felt about me.. They didn't consider me to be different no matter how long it took me to get my points across. As a matter of fact I learned how to laugh at my past as it related to my imperfection. My head would vibrate and my neck would become strained when I was stuck on a word or a phrase. I felt as though someone was constantly plugging and unplugging my vocal chords and I would grow increasingly frustrated. It wasn't funny when it was happening but I was finally able to find humor in the situation. In fact, I found that when I can laugh at myself first it almost immediately halts laughter from anyone else because I'm completely fine with it. Now that I discovered a way to accept it I no longer felt defeated and deflated when someone was careless enough to hurl an insult my way. Why should I? They are simply discovering something that I had already known and have already come to own as part of my character.

You will come to find that same joy and power that comes from acknowledging and accepting your imperfections. As a result, you will also discover just how perfect you always were; for yourself. I remember the countless opportunities that I had turned down in the past because of my immobilizing fear of ridicule and shame. There were times whereby I felt I did nothing at all but just exist and blend in with the walls. I was the shrinking violet who painfully watched everyone else around me communicate with ease. My stuttering had such an impact on me that my life goals were mostly influenced by it. I had a desire to be an actor but realized that in order to do that I'd have to speak in public. So, that dream went unfulfilled. I also had dreams of becoming a jazz singer but feared that I would mess up a word or a line, which too became a distant memory. This type of self-degradation of my goals and dreams would go on for years before I would realize just how detrimental it was to my personal happiness.

As a child I always had an active imagination. At the age of seven I wrote a song with my cousin, Darlene entitled "Journey". She and I recently recalled this episode of our lives with extreme laughter. The song was absolutely horrible but what she did not know, until recently, was that for me this song indicated a freedom of the voice that was always stuck in my head. I definitely had something to say and I needed to get it out so I began writing my thoughts.

What began as a simple means of communicating with others, as well as journaling my thoughts, would become one of the most meaningful aspects of my life. After that point, I continuously wrote songs and poems, eventually graduating to composing short stories and plays. Near the end of my 10th grade year in high school I won an award in my English class for my overall writing achievements. I had written what was considered the best short stories, plays, and poems that year in that particular class. While I was happy to have received the accolade I was still in the midst of the darkness that was created by how I felt about my imperfections. I wasn't strong enough to realize that someone was giving me an honor that no one else in my class would receive. I recall shyly accepting the award and thinking how badly I wanted to evaporate into total invisibility and make it back to my desk without vomiting, as a result of fear. Ironically, I became a writer because of my need to effectively communicate in a way that my speaking voice would not allow. So, in essence, I made wonderful accommodations for the deficiency placed upon my life. The problem was that I was not equipped to recognize that my gift gave balance to my deficiency, which in turn, made me a complete person. Remember that I previously stated that God never grants you a deficiency without granting you an equally, if not more, profound efficiency. It just took me nearly three decades to realize it.

I was totally ignoring every other attribute that provided balance to not only my life but also my place on this huge playground we call Earth. By not acknowledging my imperfection I had no way of truly discovering alternate means that would get me to the same destination. Yes, I knew that my speech impediment did not afford me the opportunity to verbally communicate as effectively as others but there were other ways that I could have achieved the same goal had I taken the time to own the issue, understand how it limited my output in one area, and discover other components of my life that I could maximize or strengthen in order to achieve my goal of getting my points across to those that matter.

There is an unspoken connection that is created when we meet people, and how our energy (which includes body language, vocal tone, and eye contact) helps to facilitate the opinions that are formed about us; often times before we mutter a single word or phrase. Even if you don't realize it, you react subconsciously to the energy of each person you encounter. Most of us will experience at least one incandescent moment that informs us that we were guilty of creating and perpetuating specific limitations. Then, we find that those same actions forced others to play along with us in terms of the limitations that they then place on us. At some point some of us will realize that playing on the negative side of our imperfections caused us to remain in victim mode whereby nothing is learned and highly effective work-arounds cannot be recognized and put into action. If you constantly tell someone what you can't do then they will usually go along for the ride because they assume you know yourself well enough to know what you can and can't do. By no means am I giving you an excuse to inflate your abilities. We all have a threshold but most of us will never push ourselves far enough to realize what those thresholds are, therefore never knowing exactly what we are capable of.

We have been surrounded by great examples of individuals living in full attendance of their life despite their limitations throughout history. Individuals without legs, whether due to accident or birth defect, find ways to complete everyday life tasks that some of us would consider nearly impossible. Blind individuals learn to master the world around them by incorporating their other senses at a higher capacity. Their sense of touch, smell, and hearing, are utilized at a higher degree than the "average" person because they have to create a healthy balance for survival. Those that are faced with certain learning disabilities find ways to make the learning process relevant and applicable to what they CAN do. Yet, some of us with comparatively miniscule setbacks cannot find the resolve that is required to move forward in celebration of the functionality that still exists for you to become as successfully as we rightfully deserve. When you acknowledge a limitation you begin to not only accept what that limitation is but you also set yourself up for the next step which involves the reorganization that is required for you to take advantage of other skills, talents, or resources that were previously ignored while walking along the "victim" path.

I once had the pleasure of hosting and co-producing The 2012 Dallas Male Author Summit. I was told by my co-producer that I should invite Desmond Blair, a digital graphic artist, as a featured artist as to bring an air of diversity to the event. I understood the vision she had for the project therefore I complied without hesitation. I am diligent about performing background research on individuals before inviting them to partake in anything that I'm associated with. So, as usual, I performed my background research on Mr. Blair and discovered that he was born with no hands. I became more curious about his functionality as it pertained to his art. As I'm sure everyone else did, I began to wonder about his creative process? Did he require any special assistance or accommodations for the event? Should I act like I don't notice that he does not have hands? How do I greet him when I'm so used to giving a powerful handshake? Did he rely on other body parts, such as his feet, to complete his projects? In hindsight I realize that some of these questions were pretty lame, as my son, Tyler, would usually say. But they are questions that I feel the average person would ask. I began to correspond with Mr. Blair as it related to the event and I found his personality, conveyed through his emails, to always have an air of positive energy and not once did he ever mention his disability. I had no idea whether he knew that I had any knowledge of it.

The day of the event, I arrived early, as part of my producer duties, to ensure that the setup was completed properly and to assist any of the authors and vendors that required any assistance or direction. I stepped outside of the venue to help another author carry his supplies when I noticed Mr. Blair standing next to his vehicle. All of the questions that I previously stated instantly began to replay in my mind. I had to regain my composure before I ended up making a complete fool of myself; which I admit to doing a few times a week. I finally made my way over to where he was so I could introduce myself. Once the introduction was made I realized that I was in the midst of God doing his work. He was naturally charismatic throughout the entire event. Visitors to his booth were afforded an opportunity to learn about his work. Again, there was not one mention of his disability because it proved not to pose any limitations to his artistic output. Later, I found out that being a graphic artist was not his only achievement. He is also a guest lecturer, motivational speaker, and entrepreneur. He had positioned himself as the perfect inspiration for those that needed to see excellence in motion that paid no regard to any shortcomings. He was in full attendance of his life because he did not allow anything to marginalize his own output nor did he allow anyone in his presence to hand him anything as result of his handicap. All trepidation I had about my current and future journey immediately dissipated. I marveled in his determination, passion, and obvious statement of defiance to any obstacles that would hinder the love of his craft and found myself wanting to stand a little taller, poking my chest out. I will go one step further and say at that moment I wanted to be more like him.

The defining moment for me was near the conclusion of the event. A young man who I assumed was in his early twenties had approached my section and read one of the flyers and noticed that I had struggled with issues related to my stuttering. We spoke for a few minutes about various topics before he revealed to me that his struggles with his hearing had left him feeling overwhelmingly self-conscious and that he even resisted learning sign language because he felt that it was indicative of waving his "white flag" of surrender. He also admitted his hesitance of wearing a hearing aid because he felt that it was the obvious sign to the world that he had a problem. I explained to him that his resistance of accepting who he was prevented him from doing what was necessary to make the best of an otherwise negative situation. I also told him that personally I felt that sign language was one of the most beautiful languages ever created and that even in silence he could communicate stories and thoughts filled with emotions that could be felt between others that he may be engaging with at the time. It was a secret language of sorts only known to few. I also explained that mastering it would also render him bilingual and create occupational opportunities that only a handful of us could fulfill. So, in turn I gave him every reason to see his submittal to the totality of his imperfection as a means of personal empowerment and expansion. Judging by the change of expression on his face I could tell that he was in full receipt of what I was saying. After our conversation he said "thank you so much for your time". Although he didn't buy a copy of my book, I felt that my words of encouragement were worth more than a few dollars. The conclusion of the event left me feeling more fulfilled than I had ever anticipated and would serve as one of the most unforgettable moments of my life up that point.

"For you formed my inward parts; you knitted me together in my mother's womb. I praise you, for I am fearfully and wonderfully made. Wonderful are your works; my soul knows it very well. My frame was not hidden from you, when I was being made in secret, intricately woven in the depths of the earth. Your eyes saw my unformed substance; in your book were written, every one of them, the days that were formed for me, when as yet there was none of them."

(Psalms 139:13-16, New King James Version)

The bible verse I quoted above was and still is a source of freedom and confirmation that assures me that every line, bump, curve, mole, and dimple is in the place that it was meant to be. Every other attribute not mentioned is also part of His divine order for my life. This confirmation also served as the first step in walking forward in my uniqueness and allowed me to reframe my thoughts about my imperfections. My opinion in regards to imperfection is that it is God's personal stamp that allows each of us to stand out amongst a crowd of billions that occupy this planet. He purposely and wonderfully created us all to be authentic and unique. Identical twins may look strikingly similar but fingerprints and other attributes separate them as completely different beings.

Your vocal tone, style of walk, and even something as simple as a protruding mole on your lip (thinking of you, Angel) can all be attributed to your unique and authentic configuration. I want you to also consider how you are able to process information (both visual and audible) in a way that speaks to the full utilization of your abilities.

No one has a right to deem you any less worthy of the fullness that life has to offer but that only happens when you understand that you have the right to demand that your authenticity be considered valuable and worthy regardless of your current situation. Remember, situations can always change but your personal value is as solid as steel. There is no one walking this earth that can fully utilize your uniqueness better than you. Recognition of this fact also results in increased personal power. It also assists in moving frames of thought away from using the label of imperfection more often and moves it closer towards uniqueness and individuality; therefore allowing you to become more celebratory within your complete self. When this happens you will notice that people will respond in kind to how you see yourself. They may not be attracted to your uniqueness but they will be attracted to the confidence that you have attached to your embracement of your uniqueness. Remember that if everyone was the same in every way then what would make YOUR presence or absence memorable? Also, consider the fact that your unique combination of physical, mental, and emotional characteristics may be just what was needed to give someone else that ray of hope and inspiration because there is someone similar to them yet still unique in their own way.

The second and most important step in my opinion, in walking forward in your uniqueness is to recognize that God's expectations for us will always outweigh the limitations we usually place upon ourselves. In fact, God does not require perfection in the physical or mental realm and it is simply because we were created with perfect intentions. That intent opens us to an exploration of means and ways that will get us CLOSE to perfect but tames us in the fact that we should never expect to be absolutely perfect especially since the idea of perfection is highly subjective if we are basing on the rule of man. For example, the highest score a judge can give during an Olympic game is a "perfect 10". The irony of the "perfect 10" is that the judge (who is man) has to feel that the contestant is WORTHY of a score of 10 based on specific rules, guidelines, as well as personal opinion. That's right. If the judge's personal conviction convinces him or her that one is not worthy of a perfect score then it is highly likely that they will not receive it. Although everyone feels that they lack something that prevents them from being perfect we are all destined for a greatness that only we could achieve using what we have been granted internally as well as the intelligence necessary to utilize external resources to the best of our abilities. You were wonderfully created in His image even though worldly events and conditions somehow has a way of slowly placing doubt within some of us that we may be either less worthy or less capable. It is at that moment you should remember that faith in your abilities and the work you put in to back that faith will eventually get you the results you want; sometimes exceedingly and abundantly.

I can remember times as a child being on the playground feeling completely invincible; letting the sandbox become the fruit of my imagination. I could be anything I chose to be at the time and no one could tell me different. Sadly, I allowed my life events to eat way at my personal innovation as I unknowingly began to lower my own standards until I basically had nothing left to strive for. But, fortunately, the limitations began to reverse over time as I began to recall the freedom of thought that was attached to the best parts of my childhood. I longed for the opportunity to play in the sandbox again, to be able to think bigger and bolder than I had imagined in a long time. Slowly but surely I began to feel my creativity return, allowing myself to see further than I had done so previously. I removed the barriers that I conceived due to what I perceived as concrete limitations. I no longer wanted to play it safe. My usual processes started to feel dated and no longer provided me with the energy I required to feel fulfilled. I decided that in order for me to become a visionary in any aspect of MY life I had to throw away some of my constraints and think beyond what I considered normal. Notice I did not use the word "abnormal" and it is because we sometimes give negative energy and definition to what we do not find comfortable and foreseeable. The area of thought that sometimes lead to slight discomfort and unfamiliarity is where we will find our highest level of creativity waiting to be set free. This is the moment that the ground below us breaks and we slowly recognize the growth that was waiting beneath our feet. Change in vision, just like any other type of change, can be scary, unfamiliar, and sometimes physically painful, depending on the goal that it applies to. But we are fully capable of allowing our imagination (that inner child) to flourish, and it is within that imagination that we create unique and manageable means of exceeding new expectations as well as creating new expectations that at one time did not seem attainable.

Creating balance within and beyond your imperfections by engaging external resources also allows one to fully maximize the utility of their imperfections. Take a blind person for example. Most of us have witnessed their use of a seeing-eye dog, or walking sticks to assists them with navigating the world. Of course they are still prone to certain vulnerabilities that the typical person with sight may take for granted but the point is that by choosing to employ resources available to them they have made the choice to live as full and productive life as anyone else. The same can be said for a person that has any other impairment such as hearing or speaking. It takes a decision, followed by actions, that creates the extension of utility that wasn't there before. By making use of available resources they are making a declaration, to the world and themselves that they want to be able to maximize their fullest potential even if some limitations exist. Of course the previous examples are somewhat extreme but I provided them to show that if people with more severe imperfections (limitations, handicaps, or any other proper classification) can make an earnest attempt to live beyond their initial limitations, then surely everyone else is capable of pushing harder and reaching further.

Though obstacles will continue to present themselves, we should accept those diversions as a means of forcing our creativity closer toward the surface of our psyche. Innovative resolutions for issues that once seemed insurmountable will then become more available, believable, and ultimately, achievable. When faced with a stop sign that originates within ourselves. Sometimes, the best thing to do is sit for a moment, rebuild the belief within, that you are fully capable and have the means and resources around you necessary to reach your goal and push through without changing course. I sometimes recognize a hindrance as a nudge from God saying "rely on everything that I have equipped you with and rely on my backing to get you past this point". Then you will realize that a hindrance along the way should never change the fact that you were always perfectly imperfect, yet fully capable of achieving everything that you desire.

"Love suffers long and is kind; love does not envy: love does not parade itself, is not puffed up; does not behave rudely, does not seek its own, is not provoked, thinks no evil; does not rejoice in iniquity, but rejoices in the truth; bears all things, believes all things, hopes all things, endures all things. Love never fails. But whether there are prophecies, they will fail; whether there are tongues they will cease; whether there is knowledge, it will vanish away"

(1 Corinthians 13: 4-8 ESV)

CHAPTER 7
WHO'S LOVING YOU?

> ***Personal Pledge:*** *Starting today, I will accept myself for who I am at this very moment. I acknowledge that I am capable of loving myself as much as I expect others to love me. I will become my own example of high self-esteem and I will command respect by showing respect for myself first.*

The thought of experiencing the joys of a perfect love affair usually conjures up thoughts of romance, adoration, and affectionate appreciation. Mentally, we instantly gravitate towards the love that is mutually shared between two people in a romantic relationship. We also tend to consider everything great that is being done to us and for us and how that affects our personal value. I thought I knew exactly what to make of love and I felt that I knew exactly how it was supposed to manifest externally and how I was to ingest it as a part of my own being. I was also very certain that my idea of what love was would provide the fulfillment, validation, and security that I yearned to feel before it came along. I spent my valuable time investing in it only to find that my investment yielded no gain whatsoever. I was to discover, in the most difficult of ways, that I had no clue as to what love was supposed to be and the fact that anything negative, dangerous, or otherwise damaging was never to be mistaken as love. I would come to suffer the deepest of heartaches because I had no idea that I could not love anyone or anything, for the right reasons, until I was able to recognize the lack of self-love that I had for myself and repair the gaping wound that had never healed properly. Sadly, I was unsure if I ever really loved myself at all up to a certain point in my life. I was not prepared for the moments that lack of self-love made a fool of me.

The years of emotional pummeling I suffered as a result of repeated sexual abuse, other physical attacks, emotional detachment from my father, the death of my first mother (my grandmother), the drug addiction of my aunt, and my severe speech impediment left me severely numb yet constantly in search of some sign of balance or reprieve. Looking back, I realized that I had spent most of my teenage and adult life seeking approval and validation from those that I felt needed the final say in my personal presentation to the world. Sometimes, I view my past as a search-and-rescue mission because I was on a constant quest to find exactly what it was about me that made me feel so inadequate and internally lonesome. Sure, I had loving friends and family members but I felt detached from them in more ways than I cared to remember. I felt as though I was playing the role of someone they liked and if they ever began to see me as I saw myself then I would surely lose all of them. When I received compliments about my intelligence I immediately gravitated towards all of the things I did not know as if to say "but, I'm not that deserving".

At the time I could not figure out why I just could not accept kind words being said about me without thinking that they were laden with ulterior and malicious motives. I didn't realize that I could not safely distinguish between compliments rendered by those that meant well and my abusers that I felt were drawn to the physical attributes for which I received the compliments. Any attention that was garnered from my physical characteristics were rejected and met with anger and distrust. I wished, at the time, that I had the ability to mute my physical presence forever. Also, when I received compliments about my looks I was only able to think of the ugly, used, and burdensome person I felt I had become. If there was a gold medal issued to the person who was best at countering every positive statement with a negative feeling then I would be the sole Olympian competing and winning the event. It was as if I believed that happiness had to come with a price tag that I couldn't afford or that I was unwilling to pay. I had a desperate need to belong and I felt that the only way that would happen is if I tried to make the people around me like me, even if it meant that I had to fabricate nearly all of who I was. I was no longer concerned with what I needed to feel complete. I was more concerned about becoming more complete and hopefully completing other people only to find out later that I was part of a damaging equation. The combination of two broken people in any capacity usually results in a very broken relationship riddled with extreme expectations and disastrous results in efforts to achieve them.

    I moved around a great deal during my childhood and teenage years. I've lived with grandparents, my mother, my father, and even my great aunt at some point in time. This resulted in my inability to form long-term friendships as well. Imagine having to reconnect with people every other year. At some point they expected me to leave just as much as I did. In essence myself and everyone around me treated me with the expectation that my presence was temporary. This is powerful because at some point I felt that my whole existence was somewhat temporary. This mindset catered to the behavior that I exhibited when I attained things. Since I wasn't going to be around long why invest fully in creating powerful bonds? I also began to develop a subconscious distrust of my surroundings and stability because I could not predict what was going to happen next. Although I have happy memories of my childhood that have somewhat helped balance the dark moments, I came to realize that the dark moments had the most profound effect on my esteem. After my grandmother died I felt displaced and out of sync. Things definitely changed and I was trying to hold on to what WAS instead of preparing for what was going to be and ultimately working towards what could have been a prosperous future for myself. I ended up being a very sensitive child and would become very disappointed in myself when my actions disappointed other people. This was also true even if I knew that the actions taken were necessary on my behalf. I developed a need to please and I cared deeply about what others thought about me. As a result of my abandonment issues I sometimes felt that I'd be sent away if I did not comply with someone's rules whether or not I felt it was right or good for me. Sometimes I'd ask to be sent to live with my mother in Louisiana in hopes of finding my place as the leader of my siblings. Moving back to Louisiana seemed to work at first but at some point it would all fall apart and I would move back to Houston. This cycle of upheaval wound up strengthening the already-dominant feelings of displacement, confusion, and a loss of belonging.

    I was shuffled back and forth from Texas to Louisiana at least every other year. I yearned to feel anchored somewhere but without my grandmother I truly felt disconnected and unprotected. I would have to attempt to rekindle the friendships that I felt were still salvageable while knowing that I did not feel worthy of being in any particular group of people. I was trying so hard to fit in without knowing or feeling confident in who I was. I'd often do very well in the beginning but then I'd revert back to being an introvert and afraid of being myself in fear of ridicule. I was also still dealing with coming to terms with my sexual abuse and the overwhelming feelings of shame, guilt, feeling used, and also feeling as if I was born to be a target for someone else's perverted desires. I was in a midst of confusion as to who I really was and that confusion would come to last for more than two decades without anyone knowing. Was I just a shell of a person filled with pitiful circumstances and occasional moments of happiness that were conditional based on who made me feel special and important? I also wondered if I was destined to be the shy kid because of my fear of speaking in public due to my severe stuttering problem. One thing was for certain and it was that I definitely was not the strong and confident person that I believed I was. All of these things slowly degraded the love I had for myself. In turn, I only loved myself as much as others loved me. Without their views of love for me I was alone and without definition. I was faceless in crowds and my voice was not to be heard even though my soul was screaming aloud and waiting to be rescued.

Several years ago, I attempted to stay in an emotionally abusive relationship primarily because I did not want to feel like a failure at love again also because the need for validation was so strong that I'd almost risk my life to keep it intact. I was prepared to deal with the abuse so long as the person was still there in some form. I knew within my heart that the love that was once there had somehow dissipated but I held on for dear life until I found myself fighting for that very same life. I would discover that my significant other at that time was just as unhappy as I was before we decided to enter into a relationship. Therefore, the only consequence was a downward spiral that included more pain and betrayal. At first, everything seemed perfect. I was showered with the level of attention that played right into my need to feel validated. Again, everything that I felt I needed were the same things that caused the relationship to falter. There were obvious signs that we were both in this for the wrong reasons and that we were each other's' catalyst for disaster. I confided my deepest and darkest thoughts about my life to this person to only have them slung back at me with such a negative amount of energy that it became completely overwhelming and unbearable. I was told that my father abandoned me because he didn't want me and that I was ugly and would never amount to anything. I truly believed that the average person would have exited the relationship a long time ago but I was willing to put my emotional well-being on the line because I did not love myself enough to make myself the priority. I had no idea that I was experiencing the lowest level of love that anyone could have for another person. I tried to make it work for all the wrong reasons. I chose to leave only when the situation could not be remedied and when I stood the chance of losing my mind as well as my life.

Immediately after the end of that relationship I literally went into isolation. We shared a home together at the time so I decided to pack only what I could fit in my 1997 Nissan Maxima and high tailed it to the nearest hotel I could afford. I would be holed up for at least two weeks all alone; once again feeling like the child that my parents left with anyone that was willing to care for me. I was jobless at the time so I was without a steady stream of income and I had not called any of my close friends to tell them of the situation. I was also in the midst of my latest bout with depression and all I felt was a need to be completely alone. I don't know whether or not I knew it at the time but it was the best thing I could have done for myself. The time alone was necessary for me to make myself the priority. I really had to decide what my next step was going to be if I was determined to make something out of all of this. The years of self-inflicted pain had finally come to a head and I had truly backed myself up against a wall. At that point I had no one to make me feel the ways that I believed I had to feel in order to justify my existence to the world. I was emptied of my companionship that I clung to for as long as I possibly could.

In the beginning of the transition out of that relationship I started to revert back to my usual feelings of loneliness and worthlessness that I felt was common for people who were not in a relationship, whether worthwhile or not. Then, I slowly began to realize that I was going through this set of painful reactions over someone that showed no regard for my painful past or my fragile future. I was beginning to make the connection that I missed for so long. I was continuing to make bad choices based on my false definition of love and self-love and my extreme desire show love coupled with my extreme lack of self-love. It had always been heavily linked to the opinions of everyone else besides my own view of myself. I did not believe that I could be alone while exhibiting a high level of self-esteem and self-worth. I made the conscious choice to bring the bad energy into my life and I had to learn how to make better choices if I wanted my quality of life to improve. Ten days after the breakup I made a promise to myself that I had never made before. I promised to not date anyone else until I felt that I was able to command a certain level of respect and stand by those commands by how I treated myself. I had to put the same level of commitment and faithfulness into my own resilience. It was time for me to learn to walk more upright with my chest poked out as I've never done before.

Have you ever found yourself hoping that you would run into someone that would turn out to be that fairytale king or queen that would somehow rescue you from all emotional and physical danger and that somehow your entire word would be a better place once he or she arrived? Sounds like a lofty expectation right? Well, it is. Not only is it lofty and overly ambitious but it is also an extremely heavy weight to place upon someone who will have a difficult enough time learning who you are merely for compatibility sake. Add on the pressure of unknowingly volunteering to be your savior will surely run a mentally well-equipped person away. Anyone that chooses to remain connected to you regardless of this problem is also questionable because your need for validation coupled with their extreme need to feel needed makes for one poisonous bowl of "what the hell is happening here" soup. The other problem with this train of thought is that until we learn to love ourselves the proper way then we are more than likely unable to recognize the components that constitute real love from someone else. This is because our receipt of love is directly connected to the love that we bestow upon ourselves and how we project this level of self-love upon others. Also, we sometimes believe the love we receive from others will act as a balance, through overcompensation, for the lack of self-love we actually feel. The truth is that no amount of overcompensation of this type can ever reconcile a low level of self-love and appreciation.

The inability to make these valuable connections allows for the blurring of the lines between unhealthy dependencies and loving someone independently of a specific need. We sometimes assume that we have fallen head over heels in love but the truth is that we are exhibiting a form of unhealthy obsession and it is the obsession that allows our tolerance level to expand to where we end up believing that we are better off having these feelings of dependency as opposed to having no one at all. In the end we realize that sometimes we accept more pain and dismay than necessary in order to simply feel attached to someone. I had to learn the hard way that it is best to want someone before you need someone. At some point you will grow to need them for specific reasons that will be revealed over time as a result of healthy communication and true compatibility.

What is the opposite effect of one's ability to identify with a high level of esteem or value? Instead of only standing in receipt of and readily accepting hurtful and disappointing situations we may find ourselves in the role of the perpetrator of pain and misery upon ourselves or others and somehow feel justified. There is truth in the statement that the way we treat others is in direct relation of what we think of ourselves. If your life has been peppered with undesirable circumstances such as abuse and neglect or even bearing witness to these actions being perpetrated against someone else at a rate that outweighs the joyous moments in your life it is easier to understand why your baseline of expectations exists more on the negative side of human relations. This baseline can also be affected by negative issues that have been ignored and therefore remain unresolved. We are sometimes conditioned to believe that what we have seen and heard is somehow acceptable. What is acceptable also becomes what is comfortable and we expect and dispense this same treatment upon others. This process usually happens after a long period of conditioning. Sometimes we have no idea that what we have come to expect or dispense has been ingrained in us since before we could even speak or comprehend what we experienced. By the time we could comprehend certain actions it was already a part of our normal program of operation.

I have fond memories of an older female cousin who I knew had a history of domestic abuse in her prior relationships. Well, she finally met what the family considered to be an upstanding guy. He was a gentleman from the outset. Even in times of turmoil he proved himself to be respectful man. He had the ability to simply walk away from heated situations without having to revert to physical or emotional violence. We as a family believed that she had finally come through her storm of bad relationships; or so we thought. One night, during a heated argument he stood up from his chair and proceeded to leave the house. He told her that he needed to be alone and wanted to go for a walk. What I witnessed next would live with me forever. I saw her chase after him. I believed that she was going to go to him and possibly resolve the issue. Instead, to my surprise, her negative behavior escalated. You could hear her arguing with him as he walked ahead of her while telling her to leave him alone.

This process continued for at least five more minutes. Then, she said to him "you not gone hit me?" It was as if she was asking for a beating. Everyone became quiet but she persisted to purposely agitate him. Her tone was insistent and you could feel the years of conditioning through her voice. He turned around in shock but remained steadfast in his refusal to lay a hand on her. She even braced herself for the impact of his hand upon her by throwing her fists up in a move as if to block an incoming punch. At first I could not comprehend it at my young age but I later came to realize that she had become so accustomed to a particular outcome that she not only expected it but she became comfortable with it. I don't believe that anyone truly wants to be abused but some of us become so accustomed to a particular type of treatment that it becomes our "normal". Anything that lies outside of that normal feels uncomfortable therefore we don't know how to receive the initial jolt of change when it happens. In this case I bore witness to an almost total depletion of self-love that had a powerfully opposite effect as opposed to someone who knew that they deserved better and demanded it.

There are others examples that can weigh heavily against our interpretation of self-love. Being exposed to a life of privilege that is not balanced with an understanding that privilege does not equate to a higher sense of self worth can also serve as an example whereby we may have created the notion that we require a certain type or amount of material possessions to feel favored by someone or to return that feeling of favor to someone else. The key to understanding self-love is looking at the word as for what it truly is, SELF-LOVE. It is one of those emotional standards in which we have complete control but usually takes us awhile to understand the power that the control can have over our entire personal system. The amount we bestow upon ourselves is affected by everything we have gone through (both positive and negative) as well as how successfully we have processed those same events. Think of it as a business that dispenses a service back to itself. We are not only the sole proprietor but also our most important customer.

The level of customer service you bestow upon yourself will be very noticeable to others and will also influence how you treat others as well. One may notice the way that you take pride in your appearance, the confident stride in your walk, or even as something as simple as the smile that you frames your face so freely without hesitation or force. These are all quiet indicators of the level of self-love/esteem that you bestow upon yourself. As a result, others who are paying the RIGHT type of attention to you are quietly engaging in a personal conversation with your actions and are sometimes making decisions on how to approach you and treat you based on the messages you relay.

Getting to the point of understanding the significance of our self-worth isn't easy for everyone. Some people live their entire lives without fully understanding the total impact, both internally and externally, that comes with not having the full understanding of the concept self-love and how to apply it as a natural way of life. This type of love exists as energy that we emit both on a conscious and subconscious level and is felt by almost everyone that comes in contact with it. It acts as a silent commander and is shown in everything from your posture, eye contact, assertiveness in your vocal tone, and even as something as simple as a handshake. At the height of positive self-love comes the "take it or leave it" attitude whereby we firmly stand by our personal guidelines and requirements for treatment and realize that others have only two choices; comply or abandon ship. Sure, it seems harsh but what other options would you prefer to have between the two? At some point the gate must either be opened or closed.

As I became more spiritually aware I came to the understanding that the basis of my creation was in fact LOVE. My spiritual growth forced me to question how strongly I believed that my creation was based on love and purpose. If I truly believe in God's plan for creating me then I also had to believe that he created me in his likeness then at the very core of my foundation is love; the ability to feel it and the responsibility to bestow it to others as He demands. Therefore I came to the stark realization that the validation I required had always been there. It was no longer something I had to seek from another human being. I was giving others the right to deem me worthy or otherwise qualified and that was a power that some wielded heavily over my life. But, I had to take the blame for giving them such power. I could no longer blame someone else for not making me feel wanted and deserving because I was always deserving of the best opportunities that this life had to offer. My lack of commitment to holding myself at a high regard trained others how to treat me. If I think lowly of myself then there was no way possible for me to begin to graciously accept kind acts of love from others.

Over time I began to unravel my own belief that self-love was some type of privilege or special attribute only possessed an elite few. I also began to understand that my level of self-awareness coupled with proper accountability and forgiveness of certain issues fed directly into my esteem. Sure, I may have believed that I needed the connection to another person to somehow make me feel more significant at a certain moment but that need to feel significant to someone else had never translated into a elevation of self-love. The same is true for everyone.

Unfortunately, some of us have to hit rock before we begin to recognize how strong a part our personal energy plays in the game of attraction of all things positive and negative. I want you to think back to the last time you were in the midst of someone that smelled of a particular scent such as a perfume or cologne. Some shy away from the smell because it may not be as pleasing to them while others are instantly drawn to it and begin to inquire about the brand and from where you might have obtained it. The love we have for ourselves resonates both inward and outward and projects a specific type of energy that some use to determine how to handle and/or treat us. Inward projection refers to the affect that self-love has on our subconscious mind. Decisions that are related to our personal well-being are directly influenced by how we feel about ourselves. Our choice in friends, mates, and what we will and will not tolerate are some of the decisions that come to mind. Try thinking of other decisions that can be directly influenced by the level of self-love you have for yourself.

Over time, these unhealthy thoughts of ourselves eventually programs our subconscious mind to believe what we think and it becomes a part of one's existence. This frame of thought prevents one from fully harnessing one's personal strength because you have already convinced yourself that you have reached your maximum potential. Then you convince yourself to just be content with where you are because the glass ceiling has been lowered to a point where there is no more room for emotional growth. This is why some of us tend to replicate problems instead of eradicating them. Such problems include dating the same people but with different bodies. Sure, they all make look different but there is an eerie connection that all of them share and it can be in the form of their own behavior or how you've allowed each of them to treat you. Then, when it is over you find yourself at the same space; blaming them for treating you a certain way without ever realizing that you chose each individual who hurt you therefore allowing self-victimization to remove any chance of self-accountability.

Our outward resonation of self-love informs others of how much we value ourselves and how we feel we measure up with the rest of the world based on what we say coupled with the actions we perform to attract what we want. If you've been told on more than one occasion that your actions don't match your words or intentions then it's time to take a hard-nosed look at how your actions affect the perception that others have of you. For example, you can't claim to be easy-going and down-to-earth if every disagreement with your opinion results in some form of melt down or antagonistic response because you feel it absolutely necessary for everyone to consider your thoughts and rationale as the bible truth.

Basically, your high or low view of yourself teaches us how to treat you based on what you consider good and fair treatment. The only two considerations from another individual is whether either comply or not with the standards you either set verbally or through your actions. If they comply with what you consider to be good and fair treatment then they can become a safe member of your emotional circle; that space within your spirit whereby what one does for and against you has a profound effect on you. If they decide that your expectations of treatment is out of scope with what they can provide then you are left with the choice to either excise them from your circle or take the big risk and allow them to stay in your safe zone. If you are able to understand the zone in question is yours to create and that you manage the adding and deleting of members of that zone you will become more self-aware of the different types of energies and personas that you are most comfortable/compatible with or not at all comfortable with. As a result, we usually only feel comfortable with people whom we feel are equally compatible on a physical, emotional, and mental level. A person with a high sense of value and esteem more than likely would not fare well in any type of personal relationship with a person that harbors low self-esteem. This is because the person exhibiting low self-esteem will most likely feel intimidated with the other person's resilience and ability to think and act independently. Oppositely, the person with the high self-esteem will become inundated by the unrealistic requirements being placed unto him or her by the other party. They will feel as though they are now responsible for their happiness as well as yours. This does not include only romantic relationships. This can include friendships, familial relationships, or even working relationships.

What it comes down to is the fact that everything we feel about ourselves will eventually come forth through our actions so it is necessary to begin reshaping our mode of thinking and reprogramming our subconscious mind to automatically enroll in a more positive way of thinking about ourselves and our life as a process that is in continual evolution even though some of us choose to believe that it stops when we decide it does by refusing not to do the work to keep up with the evolution. The best way to begin this process is taking the time necessary to become reacquainted with ourselves in a way that is mentally intimate. What happens to some of us over time is that we become accustomed to seeking validation and acceptance from external people or resources and confusing it with self-love. This void, once filled or partially filled, becomes the center of happiness for the individual but so little of the void actually contains anything that pertains to the individual. Thus, in the absence of those external people of resources, the void reappears. Does this sound like a familiar feeling after the loss of an important relationship? The pain of losing a meaningful relationship is normal and expected but to go so far beyond that feeling and have it transform into a feeling of worthlessness is the tell-tale sign that we allowed someone or something the privilege of wielding too much power over the perception we have of ourselves. We must now attempt to fill the void with characteristics about ourselves that make us feel more complete and noteworthy.

How does the lack self-love manifest itself within our lives? There are several noticeable characteristics that may be present and it differs from person to person. I took the liberty to create a list of what I feel are common attributes associated with the level of self-love one may exhibit. This list was culminated from years of self-observation and the observation of others at varying stages of their lives and I feel it is important for you, the reader, to discover what you may find in common with the list being presented.

LOW ESTEEM	HIGH ESTEEM
Higher level of dependence within interpersonal relationships. Also, there is a higher possibility that ideas and beliefs are easily influenced by others.	Possesses the ability to maintain individuality within interpersonal relationships as well as being able to effectively express their ideas.
Higher level of tolerance for unhealthy actions (whether committed by self or others)	Able to recognize when actions are not conducive to overall happiness
Higher propensity and need for instant gratification (i.e. whirlwind romances, monetary indulgences, and drug and/or alcohol)	Recognizes the value of patience as it relates to both short and long-term goals. Also, there is a clearer understanding of consequences related to some forms of instant gratification.
Lower expectations of achievement and success	Very well-thought-out plan of action for achievement and recognition where change is important
Feelings of extreme inadequacy	Recognizes their positive uniqueness and strives to be better for themselves initially
Lack of motivation for personal development	Very proactive in their personal development and is usually more forward-thinking in their efforts

While observing this chart you may find some familiarity with either side of the spectrum because the manifestation of our self-love is unique to us and this chart represents the characteristics found in either extreme. Your personality may actually lie somewhere in the middle but what is important is that you make the connection that allows you to recognize how much work is required of you. We want to work towards being nearer the highest level of self-love and self-regard and maintain those practices and activities that will keep us there. Understand that certain events in life will happen that will cause us to deviate between the levels but once you are able to attain a higher sense of self-awareness you will find that your ability to persevere through those situations will be strengthened and that you are able to bounce back much quicker than before. Also, you will be able to make more rational decisions during stressful times because you will have learned to trust yourself enough to know what is best for who you are as an individual.

At times it is perfectly fine to become selfish and require the personal time required to fully invest in your quest to discover what makes you unique and focusing of the positive aspects of your uniqueness. Once the rediscovery is complete then the stage is set for learning how to love yourself from the inside out. The rediscovery process, for me, was a seemingly lonesome one. I literally had to force myself to make time to spend time by myself to understand what made me happy, what made me angry, and what I could and could not tolerate from myself. This is important because what we will and will not tolerate from ourselves is usually identical to what we will and will not tolerate from others. I realized that I slowly lost my love of literature so I began to frequent a local Barnes & Noble bookstore by myself. I would pull various books from the shelves, order either a cappuccino or latte, take a seat, and skim over books for what seemed like hours. I discovered that I enjoyed peace and quiet and that I seemed to function better in small and intimate crowds. I also found a love for a certain category of novels. I involved no one else in this process because I wanted it to be as unfiltered and uninfluenced as possible and I so desperately wanted to learn to enjoy my own company. Once I achieved this I realized that I now was able to say that I genuinely like myself. Yes, there was more work to be done but at that point I liked the person that I was becoming and was looking forward to more growth in the near future. What my loneliness and sense of void was replaced with a growing level of self-respect and appreciation for who I really was. I was intelligent, caring, comical, and fun-loving and it had nothing to do with anyone else being in my life at that particular time.

If you are at a point where you dispute your own level of self-love then I urge you to begin your process of discovery by imposing a period of self-invoked isolation that will allow you the opportunity to learn and love who you truly are that is absent of major influence by other parties and things. It is simply taking the required time to become completely comfortable in your aloneness and accepting that, at times, the alone time is perfectly fine and is one of the best opportunities for truly listening and reacting properly to everything else around you. The end result of this isolation can teach you more about yourself as well as enforcing your freedom from external sources of happiness. I used my trip to a local bookstore chain as an example but this can be done in the comfort of your own home or anywhere you feel you thrive as an individual. I usually suggest to others that it is best to start by taking part in activities that you can do alone and requires you to sit and think about who and what you believe you are. Granted, certain activities require the participation of one or more additional parties so you're going to have to know when it is time to be alone and when it is time to showcase everything that you've learned about yourself to others.

Try doing things such as going to the movies alone, having coffee alone at your favorite coffee shop while reading that book you've been dying to get your hands on. Taking yourself on a road trip to a relaxing destination can also serve the same purpose. The one thing that all of these activities have in common is that they are enjoyable to YOU and that you do not need permission from anyone or have to feel included in a particular number or a special group of people because YOU are the most important person in the group of ONE. No one else is influencing what you are choosing to read, drink, watch, or wear. In addition, no one is dictating to you those things that you should be able to decide for yourself. Also, no one else is there to make you feel as though your choices are inadequate. In addition, these choices help you to discover and define your true personality. You will more than likely discover qualities about yourself that you never knew existed or that you never paid much attention to but actually enjoy. You may also discover that certain things tug at your heart that may not mean much to anyone else. The opportunity has been presented for you to own what is part of your being and celebrate whatever it is that adds to the collection of great qualities that you have been ignoring for so long. So often we expect to have an epiphany that contains monumental findings but the love for yourself is found in the smallest of details and once we learn to appreciate the smallest of details then we successfully graduate to understanding that the smaller details contribute to the larger details. In fact, the larger details of your life are a composite of the smaller details.

Now that you've taken the time to understand the importance of discovering the finer details of what can contribute to your overall happiness it is time to allow yourself the opportunity to play up your strong points, and at the same time recognize where work needs to be done but without suffering the penalty that you may usually inflict upon yourself. That penalty usually begins and ends with self-doubt. Don't be afraid to give yourself credit when no one else does. Not everyone will appreciate your various contributions to this world and not everyone will like you. Working to appeal to everyone is a fruitless effort because their personal requirements of you may change at will which will result in additional chaos and the only person that suffers in the end is you. I usually tell people that I know that I am a genuinely good person and that I only care what certain people think about because they actually matter and have an important role in my life. Otherwise, I would have to trust that most people recognize my positive attributes and judge me accordingly. But, I no longer care to find out what the majority thinks and that most of what I do is deeply rooted in what I feel is best according to my personal needs.

We have to understand that although there are billions of humans on this earth we are unique in some form or fashion. Sometimes our lack of self-love is a precursor to a larger feeling of inadequacy or lack of uniqueness. It is human nature for humans to cycle through comparisons against others. It often takes us several cycles of these comparisons to the attributes of others before we realize that we will always find at least one person that seems to possess an attribute that is stronger than our own. Some of us wish to be taller, shorter, thinner, thicker, more athletically inclined, more studious, more romantic, and even more sympathetic. Some of these attributes can be developed over time but the bottom line is that we have to come to understand that who we are today is worth celebrating just as much as who we wish to become tomorrow and forward.

I slowly began to learn how not to attach my goals and dreams to what others felt I should be doing with my life. When your esteem is high you are able to convey your convictions with confidence and are proud to be able to speak confidently about what matters most to you. More than likely, I would have completed my college degree much sooner had I followed my heart instead of following recommendations from other people. I know that my best interest was at the heart of their discussions about my future but no one supported what I felt was the natural progression of my life and the aspirations tied to those goals. Since my belief in myself was at an all-time low I went with the flow and felt that everyone else was able to make better decisions about my life than I was. Granted, I still feel that I should always listen to valuable opinions but still retain the freedom to make my own decisions based on all of the information that is presented. I speak about forming and relaying expectations later in the book but it is important to know that without self-love there is a lack of confidence that will dissuade you from stating what you want and need from others in order to sustain healthy and balanced relationships. Once again, our goal is to grant ourselves permission to love who we are and what we stand for from within and allow the confidence that comes from this new level of self-appreciation to radiate outward where others can take notice and react to us accordingly.

Choose today as the day that you begin to honor yourself and to feel beautiful about the body and the spirit that you were blessed to have. This type of honor includes honoring your thoughts and feelings as being important enough for yourself and everyone else to respect. Learn to tell yourself the ultimate truth and that is that you are worthy of all the respect, love, and adoration simply because you are God's child. Notice I didn't say that you will be worthy. I am telling you to live in that moment as if it is already here. By doing so you are a slowly programming your subconscious mind to behave as if what you desire has already been granted. If you think you are less than deserving then you will always behave as such; therefore allowing others to treat you as such. You are not required to be in a place of total love and peace in order to enjoy the benefits of having a high esteem. These are the moments where you can justify having a selfish attitude and as a result, learning to command that honor from others by displaying it in everything that you do. Allow the upright posture of your walk define your character while your effortless confidence dictates how you ought to be treated.

    During our lifetime, some of us forget to pay ourselves back for the hard work and commitment that's required to sustain our mental stability. You usually here this type of talk from a financial analyst but I'm speaking in regards to paying yourself the compliments that you expect others to give. Adore yourself in a way that brings forth a level of self-worth and acceptance that is not predicated on anyone else's belief in your right to receive such adornment. Eventually, you will come to take pleasure in the control you possess in regards to how you view yourself and how the majority of the world will view your presence. Surprise assumptions will be minimal because you will already know what others have yet to learn. If you know that you are a person that prides themselves on helping others then learn to appreciate yourself for it even if the "Thank You's" are far and few between. You may be the person that possesses a great skill that the world has yet to witness. Keep at your craft and reinforce your learning by acknowledging each successful step as a step in the right direction and appreciating each setback as an opportunity to learn to do things wiser the next go round. Grant yourself the permission to be happy with who you are at every stage of growth instead of awaiting that monumental and overwhelming moment of clarity that truthfully may never come, especially if it is dependent on someone else taking notice. It's about time you become your own best cheerleader.

INTERMISSION III: *The Love Letter; Your Personal Greeting Card*

Certain life events present us with the opportunity or the desire to bestow upon others kind words of gratitude and appreciation. On the other hand we may also feel the need to communicate other sentiments with words; both written and oral. My oldest son is fascinated with greeting cards and the different sentiments that can be expressed with each one that he surveys. One thing that I noticed is that there isn't a greeting card specifically designed for us to give to ourselves as a means of acknowledgment, gratitude, or simply to say how much one loves him or herself in a confirming way. *The Love Letter* provides the moment for you to do just that; to give yourself permission to applaud and confirm the reasons why you should now and always love yourself despite life's circumstances and any inadequacies that you feel may have diminished your personal outlook.

The Love Letter asks you to write a letter to yourself honoring the attributes that make you worthy of receiving the highest level of adoration. The same adoration you are able to bestow upon yourself is directly related to the ways that you bestow love upon others. It takes into consideration no wrong doings or negative judgments. However it does take into consideration your positive treatment of others and allows you to see how you truly feel about yourself at this point in time. No compliment is over the top in this exercise. Be as creative and thought provoking as you can. Use phrases such as "I love myself because" as a way of framing your thoughts about yourself. Also, consider why you feel other people love you even if you initially have a hard time believing it. Finally, consider your spiritual foundation. Consider that God loves you for the same reasons that you should love yourself. Allow yourself the opportunity to brainstorm freely about self-love without apology or discretion. Consider this letter as a gift to yourself from yourself.

The only prerequisite for this process is that you find a quiet and positive space that is as free of distractions as possible.

Begin the letter by inserting your name in the blank field below to assert that this is specifically for **YOU**:

Dear _____ (insert your name)

Next, begin the self-adoration process. As mentioned before you can begin the letter with the phrase "I love me because" and allow the words to flow freely. You can stop and start as many times as you feel but try your best to find as many reasons that you can to adore YOURSELF.

_____
_____
_____
_____
_____
_____
_____
_____
_____
_____
_____
_____
_____
_____
_____
_____
_____
_____
_____

Love,

_____ (sign your name)

Now, I want you to read your letter back to yourself and answer the following questions:
1. Were you able to define more reasons to love yourself as initially thought?
2. How did you feel as you were writing the letter?
3. Did the writing process evoke any positive memories that you may have forgotten?
4. How did you feel as you read the letter back to yourself?
5. Has this process invigorated your desire to continue to explore the reasons why you are deserving of the highest level of self-love and adoration?

CHAPTER 8

FROM DESIRES TO DESERVEDNESS

> ***Personal Pledge***: *I understand that the way I lead my life dictates the feedback that I receive as a result of my actions. My desire for success requires me to think and live in a way that is conducive to attracting and attaining all that which I desire.*

I can remember a point in time just a few years back when I used to complain to myself about things that I had yet to achieve. These complaints included not making the money that I should be making in my career as well as not being able to attract what it was that I desired. I wanted to use my talent to help others overcome adversities and lending to the bottom line of personal advancement but had no idea how to channel my desire and create opportunities to fulfill what I felt was one of my duties in life. There is a great deal of truth when it is implied that we have the ability to attract what we desire and it is not merely based on the energy that we conduct but also based on our behavior and how we project our desires into the world.

How many times have you heard a family member or friend complain about not having enough money or not being able to find and/or keep a good man/woman in their lives? If you are like me then the answer is "way too many times". Then, at moments I saw myself through their frustrations. I had been in only a handful of relationships but most of them ended very unsuccessfully. Was it their fault or mine that it did not prove successful? At this point in my life I can honestly say that it was a combination of the two. At times I was the main culprit and there were times where I was the one that gave people a free pass to hurt me. Part of it was because I felt that that is what I deserved based on what I had been through in the past. I may repeat this passage more than once in the book but we have to learn to not let our past or current condition dictate our overall purpose in life.

I began to look at most of the actions that led me to that point in my life where I just didn't feel as though I was doing the things that I should be doing. Also, I began to look at how I treated people in general. I'm usually a kind and warm-hearted person so I couldn't really say that it was because I didn't attempt to plant seeds of kindness. I did notice, however, that I wasn't taking care of ME. I failed to make myself the priority in most equations and it was because I was more concerned about how I made others feel. I worried about if I disappointed someone or if I was doing what was necessary for someone to like me even if it meant doing things that I did not enjoy. I used to feel that the person I dated was to be the one to solve every problem that existed before they arrived. I looked for approval from people in a most disturbing and co-dependent way. I did not have much of anything to propel myself to the next level of greatness. In fact, every movement in my life was a lateral move, different scenery but same circumstances so long as it was a scene that was comfortable. I hadn't seen an upward bound movement within myself in years. What I had to understand is that I am entitled to greatness even before I made a fair attempt to attain it. Our greatness is there for us to receive but it only arrives when we take the necessary steps that cause us to expect it, draw it to ourselves, and maintain it.

To expect greatness is to first believe that it will come to you and that you actually deserve it. When I speak of greatness I am speaking in the most general of terms. It's not specific to a certain set of accomplishments but more so relates to the concept that you should expect the maximum level of achievement so long as you perform the work that is necessary. It is extremely difficult to predict greatness when it seems as though your life has been riddled with hardships that you couldn't control or remedy. Growing up for me wasn't always easy when I dealt with the residual effects of sexual abuse, neglect, and what felt like abandonment, but I could not see past those events no matter what else transpired. I made great grades in school and won numerous awards and contests in school based on my writing skills. I was able to transport myself and others into perfect worlds or stretch their imagination with the magic of my words. I felt joy as I wrote my fantasies about being a different person, living in a different world, and undergoing totally opposite circumstances. Still, I focused on the grim times and allowed those thoughts to override the thoughts that would have convinced me that I was worthy of so much more. As a result, I began to behave in a manner that no longer dictated greatness but settled for middle-of-the-road or even sub-standard results. So, I had decided that I didn't deserve more than what I had ever gotten and that my goal was to merely survive instead of prospering. Funny thing is that I had always desired more but was still resigned to the fact that I didn't deserve it. I was once again resigned to my safety zone which included not confronting the problems I faced or even confronting myself in a way that would force me to relearn what I thought I knew of myself.

How do we convince ourselves that we deserve the best that life has to offer? I asked myself that question for years. The answer didn't come to me until I slowly began to uncover the various sources of my issues. I discovered that most of my life was being controlled by elements over which I had no control. I had somehow blamed myself for everything that had happened so it was impossible for me to expect the rewards of living a full life if I was constantly blaming myself for anything negative that had ever transpired in my life.

This is why self-blame can be our worst enemy because it cripples our ability to see ourselves in any other light but a dark and foggy one.

I needed to learn how to rightfully demand the respect I desired from others without seeming forceful or belligerent. I had to find that balance of confidence and self-respect that would be noticeable by most that I encountered. Then, I was more than likely to receive respect in return. Even those that did not like me would be subliminally forced to at least pay me the respect that I paid to them. Because I had lost confidence and some respect for members of my family I truly had to live as my own example of respect. It's an old saying but it's very true that no one will respect you until you respect yourself. These elements were missing from most of my personal relationships which would explain why my feelings were dismissed so easily and that hateful actions against me were repeated without remorse. I learned that some people will do to you what you allow them to do and some back down once you display the type of resilience that is powerful and unwavering.

Self-respect, or lack thereof, can have a resoundingly negative effect on how way others view and interpret your character. If you are careless with the level of respect you give to yourself it can easily be seen as a welcome mat for others to take advantage of you. It is a sad reality that some people do prey on the insecurities and instabilities of others and sometimes we have no idea that their motives are so manipulative and disastrous. Once we show a particular level of carelessness we then lose all reasoning to question why certain people betray us. But, is it really betrayal if we invite the betrayal by appearing to be open to and ok with it? I've witnessed many relationships, including my own, crumble under very extenuating circumstances but it was usually the result of not being mindful of why and how we entered into those relationships.

I can admit to spending way too much of my valuable time blaming the other person when things became disastrous in the relationship. These relationships can include family, friends, associates, work, and even love. The fact is that all relationships are built on at least two endpoints, yours and the other person's. The easiest way to receive respect within any relationship is to first exude a high level of self-respect, even if you have yet to attain it. You have now created a blueprint by which others must treat you. It is the same blueprint that you must also follow at all times because your self-treatment has to be consistent before others buy into it. Also, allow room for the blueprint to change but only in a positive direction. Then, you will find that other self-respecting individuals will be drawn to you because they know that if you have high regard for yourself then you should more than likely have high regards for your fellow man.

How does self-respect relate to deserving what you desire? Simply put, a high level of self-respect leads you to a place where you become your primary focus when necessary. Combined with elevated confidence, your aspirations now matter a great deal more than they did in the past because they are now seen as attainable goals. You now know the difference between simply dreaming and planning for success. At that point you will come to realize that you are worthy of greatness in whatever measurable capacity. This is another perfect opportunity to act somewhat selfishly towards gaining the self-respect you deserve. It begins with understanding that you are no less deserving than the person standing next to you. They may have been lucky enough to be born into a family that has more financial means or a seemingly better social class than you but that by no means distinguishes them as being better than you. The trick is for you to learn to believe and remember it when it is necessary.

A dream of mine was to become a jazz singer. No one knew of this dream and I call it a dream because at the time I honestly felt that it was just that. I had no true belief within myself that I could actually become a jazz singer. Maybe the fantasy helped me to temporarily escape the harsh realities that I was dealing with at the time. I was unable to fathom that the dream could be reality and it was primarily because I felt that I did not deserve such a blessing. For some reason I felt that I was unable to reach a point in my life where my wildest dreams would ever become a reality. Internally, I hurt myself with such thoughts because I was forcing myself to remain at a particular level of non-achievement all throughout my life. My family knew that I was intelligent but I felt average compared to others. It wasn't because of anything anyone had done. It was because I did not feel as though I could compete with their esteem and their heightened sense of confidence.

This concept also plays a great role in how we behave in our personal relationships. Often times we find ourselves, or others, demanding certain things from a relationship but not understanding that we play a much larger role in what others feel we deserve and what others give to us. It is so true that most people do to us what they feel we expect of them or whatever they can get away with. A lack of self-confidence presents a surefire entrance of unwanted repercussions such as emotional and physical abuse as well as alienation. Once the door is opened it becomes harder to close because each strike to our physical or mental body creates a wound that usually grows wider and deeper before it begins to heal. Just like any wound it has to go through the process of healing slowly. This is when your belief that you are worthy of success comes into play. Obstacles will present themselves at the most inopportune of times but as long as you display a consistent, if not elevated, sense of determination and self-worth you will come you will see a noticeable change during your recovery process. Your success will consist of ordered steps that are directly related to what you feel in your heart is rightfully yours.

What happens when the opposite takes place and we feel that we deserve things that we truly hadn't earned? We hear it all the time from people we know. A woman may say that she deserves a good man but isn't living life in a way that would draw an ideal candidate for a husband. A man may say that he deserves to be wealthy but isn't doing anything to push him towards that mark of wealth or is waiting for the financial heavens to open up and rain upon him. My opinion is that these types of people have an exaggerated view of their self-worth and live in the mode of "receive now, pay later," or a sense of entitlement. This type of view makes it either difficult or impossible for the recipient to feel a sense of satisfaction that comes from hard work.

The hard work I speak of consists of first positioning yourself to believe that you are capable of great achievements. This capability isn't something that comes out of nowhere but is recognized when you've created a plan for success, which includes utilization of resources to help you reach your goal. The goal is to become deserving of your desire by doing the work that is required to recognize opportunities as they present themselves. Sometimes, we are put in the path of achievement but we are unable to recognize it or are frightened because it is a change in the way we usually do things. If you condition yourself to believe that you deserve greatness based on the fact that you are entitled to it as an occupant of this earth as well as being rewarded for your extended efforts investing the time and energy required for you to rebound with a newfound level of joy and satisfaction.

This requires commitment on your part. I suggest that you enlist the help of people who you feel will hold you accountable and will offer positive reinforcement and encouragement when necessary. The support system you create becomes invaluable throughout this process not only because they will hold you accountable but also because you will know from which parts of your support system to lean on. Those whom you lean on should remind you that you are indeed deserving of the best especially when during those times that you feel otherwise. I can honestly admit to having at least three days a week that are filled with self-doubt. I go through the usual cycle of asking "why me"? I reiterate to myself everything that I have done up to this point and reminding myself that even if I had not done anything at all that I would still be deserving of the best that life has to offer. Those that appear strong always have their moments of self-doubt. The only difference between you and them is that they know how to deliver themselves out of that rut and to continue to along their path of greatness.

I can honestly say that my moments of greatest clarity, as it relates to being worthy of greatness, revealed themselves about two or three years ago. I admit that it was a very laborious process to attempt to reinvent my way of thinking. I believe they say it takes 14-21 days to form a habit. That is so true. My way of thinking had to become mechanical before it was to become automatic. I wrote little notes and emails to myself. I'd also write encouraging taglines in my emails so that I could share it with others. Even with going back to school and raising a son I still had a few reasons to doubt my ability to be successful. As my outlook changed so did the outlook of others towards me.

Then, there is the magic of believing the opinion of the majority. Have you ever had a situation where you were offered a very positive compliment or an opportunity that could really make a very noticeable impact on your life and you just couldn't bring yourself to believe that you deserved it? How about when several people tend to bestow upon you the same compliments or opportunities and you are still afraid to believe that it could be true? This could mean that you have yet to recognize that you've always done the work that was necessary and that you are finally being justly rewarded for your efforts. But the awards are as meaningless to you as the sentiment by which you perceive it to be offered to you.

A prime example of this comes from my own story of how I got into radio production. Prior to this happening I was still plagued with insecurities related to my speaking voice. Sure, I had overcome a great deal of the adversity associated with my stuttering. I was able to effectively express my opinion without fear of what others would think about how I spoke. I was also able to increase both my esteem and self-worth. Also, someone thinks I have what it takes to actually speak to hundreds of people. I initially avoided the urges of a few of the people in the business because I honestly did not share the same sentiment. Over the course of a year I realized that my goal was to use my adversities as a tool to help others. I had already become a certified coach practitioner and began to function as a life coach so, in part, I was fulfilling this destiny. Now, I was faced with the opportunity to create something that would allow me to reach much more people. It wasn't until then that I began to realize that I was receiving exactly what I had always wanted which was an opportunity to follow my destiny. But, I almost denied myself the privilege because I had not programmed my mind to believe that I could do it.

I was offered an opportunity to co-host an ITunes-radio talk show during the early part of 2009. I had made up my mind that I would not pass over another opportunity so I took the offer and began writing and recording test segments. I was the "life coach" of the talk show and I have to admit that being able to research and apply a life coaching methodology to everyday problems felt exhilarating and highly purposeful for me. I was learning the ins-and-outs of how to write for radio. The pilot of the show only lasted for a few weeks before it was disbanded due to creative differences between the executive producer and the general manager. Prior to the disbandment I was approached by the general manager and was told that I had what it took to have my own show and was even compared to the likes of Oprah Winfrey. I was highly flattered and elated. I felt that my education and personal development was finally paying off but the general manager could tell that I still required some coaxing. I decided to allow his belief in me serve as the driving force to this new creative outlet. We started the development of my own show but things did not go as planned so we canned the project. Overall, the experience itself planted seeds of creativity within me that I realized could no longer lay dormant. I decided to own my talent by creating my own production company that would handle all of my multimedia endeavors including my own radio show as well as this book that you are reading at this very moment.

I said all of this in hopes that you understand that everyone, including you, has a voice and a talent that can be used to create opportunities and circumstances that provide inspiration for others while also furthering your own level of advancement. We can learn to allow our passion to balance our lives by providing a sense of enjoyment that is energizing and reassuring. My voice was muffled not only as a result of my circumstances but also because I believed that my current circumstances dictated where I would later end up in my life. I had to learn that I was deserving of everything that my heart desired but I first had to believe that I deserved it, act as if I had already earned it, and prepare myself to welcome the opportunities that would come as a result of my diligence. I had to learn that once my voice was discovered that it was my God-given right to sing as loudly as I can because the right people will eventually listen.

CHAPTER 9

THE TRUTH ABOUT EXPECTATIONS

> **Personal Pledge:** *I will learn to set my expectations as high as reasonably possible while respecting the realms of my reality. I will not burden myself or others with unattainable expectations and I will learn how to make my expectations known so that I may hold myself and others accountable when necessary.*

The huge elephant has now entered the room, messed up your perfectly laid flooring, and has decided to sit smack dab in the middle of the room for a spell. Now, you have no choice but to acknowledge the elephant's presence. The only two choices is either call your local animal control agency or allow it to stay as long as IT desired. Either way, a decision must be made on how to deal with the elephant we call EXPECTATIONS.

It's been my recent experience that the word "expectation" has become one of the most frightening words to use as it relates to personal relationships. Some feel that it places undue pressure or hardship on the other party while some feel that it's best to create lofty goals and aspirations without ever taking into consideration upon whom they are placing these expectations upon.

How many times have you found yourself disappointed or let down by the actions of another person? How many times have you felt that it was entirely their fault? There comes a point in time where we have to question our expectations as to whether or not they are rational and even attainable. We also have to realize how our expectations play a part in our own frustration. But, overall, expectations are very much required in order to find balance in our dependence on people and resources.

Expectations are things and actions that we look forward to or what is expected and they exist at almost every level of our existence. We create expectations mostly at a subconscious level based on the role of a particular thing or individual and can be influenced by culture, religion, or any other value system. We expect certain functions from our television and other equipment just as we expect certain things from individuals. The roles of husband and wife carry certain expectations that may differ from the role of boyfriend and girlfriend. Our sisters and brothers hold us to different expectations as they do their best friends. So, it is fair to say that every role in life comes with preconceived expectations that we feel obligated to meet or that we place on others to have met. The danger lies in our inability to form realistic expectations, thus setting ourselves up for failure or heartbreak.

The most important expectations are those that we place upon ourselves. We hope that these expectations are healthy and are in line with our abilities so that we may be able to meet most of them, if not all. But, in the midst of pain and confusion we can easily become misguided in our efforts to meet certain expectations. As a result of controversy we sometimes expect ourselves to be resilient at times when we should succumb to the effects of pain and disappointment. If not, we stand the change of further delaying our release from pain. We have to allow ourselves the opportunity to go through the cycle of hurt, revelation, diagnosis, and healing in order to fully appreciate the significance of our struggle. This becomes difficult when we hold either very low or very high expectations of ourselves.

Expectations can be compared to a set of stairs that start at one level and end at a level that is higher than the first but lower than the next. Each expectation can be seen as a step towards something better, the next level. As we meet expectations we should progress to bigger and better expectations that lead us to the next level of achievement. Sometimes, the process becomes interrupted by negative thoughts and perceptions and we find ourselves either standing in place or repeatedly falling backwards attempting to surpass that next level.

I remember a time where my expectations for myself were both so low and so high that I am very surprised that I was not suicidal. In the midst of understanding the abuse I suffered and my fear of abandonment I was resigned to the thought that my life was restricted to just those actions and that anything better was out of my reach. I wore my feelings on my sleeve and they existed in every word that I spoke so it was no surprise that I was attracting people and doing things that contributed to those low expectations. I needed to feel wanted even if the feeling came from those that I really did not care for. I also wanted my presence to count for something as opposed to nothing at all. With low and unrealistic expectations in tow, I was spiraling dangerously out of control within myself and felt ok with that. Once I met those expectations I just repeated them. I fell backwards a few times but rarely did I ever surpass a particular level and when I did it frightened me to pieces because I was not expecting better and felt that something had to be wrong. There was no growth plan nor was there any other way for me to pull myself out of the rungs of my despair. I fooled myself into believing that it was ok only because I was too lazy and absorbed in sorrow to do anything about it.

These unhealthy expectations brought consequences such as destructive habits and relationships that I tried to either justify or blame entirely on someone else. I was quick to blame everyone and everything besides myself. I was slow to realize that I was the common denominator in all of my problems. This is not by any means taking any fault away from the people who inflicted harm on me in my past. This is more of a way to hold myself accountable for present and future actions and reactions. I had to almost lose everything to find myself. I grew so tired of subjecting myself to mental and verbal abuse and the constant berating of myself that I had no choice but to finally look upward and beyond what I ever had attained. There was no immediate ray of hope yet there was angst to test the waters for the first time. I can attest to the power of self-expectations.

For me, the expectations changed once I came to terms with my life as it was. At some point we all have to be realistic and ask ourselves "where is my life going right now?" Consider all of your habits, both positive and destructive and map the conclusions of what you anticipate. For example, if you are in and out of dangerous relationships then the conclusion is that you may end up dead or severely wounded, either mentally and/or physically. If you are moving from location-to-location with no real purpose you may realize that you are attempting to run away from problems that you thought you were able to leave behind. So, your expectations cannot be far off from your current actions or any future actions that you plan to partake in. You can't plan to be happily married if going in and out of volatile relationships nor can you expect to live a stable and secure life if your actions lean toward an evolving door of cities and faces.

I firmly believe that everyone possesses a skill or attribute that can define them in a positive sense. Sometimes, we need to remember that or keep it close to our hearts when we feel the need to lay judgment upon ourselves. Our expectations are partly based on the judgment we place on ourselves so if we began with an unhealthy judgment then we will end up with unhealthy expectations. Statements such as "I expect to fail" will foil every attempt you make to not fail because the mind remembers your fears and acts upon them at the point that you wish it does not. Now, you have to work harder at attempting to pass as opposed to preventing failure. Statements such as "I will pass" reprogram the subconscious mind to think of passing as the initial goal while attempting NOT to fail. It goes back to the statement of seeing the glass half full or half empty. Our circumstances and environment create our conditioning, which in turns programs how our subconscious mind creates expectations. There is safety in being somewhat pessimistic but being overly pessimistic sometimes stifles progress.

I want to take this time to introduce an activity that I feel will bring the appropriate recognition the expectations that we place upon ourselves and others. Below I have included what I call the EXPECTATION WORKSHEET.

EXPECTATION WORKSHEET:

EXPECTATION	RATING	WHAT NEEDS TO HAPPEN?	ADDITIONAL RESOURCES	IS IT REALISTIC?
To be more outgoing with my peers	8	I need to build my confidence so that I can feel as though I am being severely judged by others.	Coaching, therapy, becoming involved in more social activities.	Yes
To find a mate to save me from my despair	7	Nothing. The expectation is unrealistic. Need to build upon my own independence and raise trust level within myself	Therapy, building a sound support system	No

This worksheet serves as a great way to introduce yourself to your own expectations. I begin by providing a column that describes the expectation, titled EXPECTATION. Next, is a column specifically for the purposes of rating the expectation (RATING). I recommend a rating of 1-10 with 10 being the highest. The columns entitled WHAT NEEDS TO HAPPEN TO refer to which tasks must be accomplished in order to meet this expectation and are more abstract such as "meeting new people" or "becoming more self-aware."

Next, the column titled ADDITIONAL RESOURCES refers to any resource that can assist you in reaching a particular expectation. Consider resources such as counseling, taking a class, or reading specifically targeted subject matter as fortification when attempting to reach these significant milestones. Finally, the column titled IS IT REALISTIC? Forces you to ask ourselves if the overall expectation is realistic and is based on the information in the previous columns.

The first expectation that I have listed is in regards to being more social with my peers. This is important because being social amongst our peers can provide great benefits such as networking for professional purposes and finding a level of enjoyment that we cannot obtain when we are alone. Also, becoming more social with peers increases your ability to be open-minded to different views. This was actually an expectation that I placed upon myself. Next, I provided a rating of 8. I felt that it was highly important but not so important that I could not live without it. The final columns are very important and should not be answered until AFTER you list all of your expectations and I will explain why in just a moment. I continued to the next line and entered the expectation of meeting a mate to rescue me from my despair and assigned it a rating of 7 which also makes this expectation seem very important.

For example purposes I would continue to list all of my expectations and assign them an initial rating. Once completed, I would then review each expectation and determine whether it was realistic or not. I advise you to list all of your expectations and ratings. Also, do not be afraid to list expectations related to others, especially if they have yet to be met. If you have a significant someone you may want to list expectations that you feel that may have been ignored. Feel free to list expectations related to friends, family members, and even co-workers. The idea is for you to show all of your cards and to capture what you are really expecting out of life. Once completed, I would like you to put away the list for at least an entire day. Give yourself time to come out of the thinking mode and let the list live on its own for some time without your intervention.

Okay, at least a day has passed and I am now ready to retrieve the list that was made yesterday. I've had time to not think about it and to approach it with a clearer point of view. Now, I begin to evaluate the expectations that I previously entered line by line. Yesterday, my focus was to just list as many expectations as I could as well as a rating. Today, my goal is to fill in the blanks of each column associated with each expectation. It is time to determine what needs to happen for the first expectation to come to fruition. I knew that it was my level of confidence and my extreme shyness that prevented me from being as social as I could have been. So, the answer was to build my confidence and lessen my fear of judgment. But, these things could not happen automatically so I had to consider additional resources to assist me such as coaching, therapy, and involving myself in more social activities. Finally, I had to determine if this goal was even realistic based on the data that I recently entered.

The next expectation gets a lot of us in trouble. Granted, this may not be an expectation that you have at the current time but we will use it to highlight an instance of an unhealthy expectation. I listed finding a mate to save me from despair as my second expectation and assigned it a rating of 7 which means that I find it to be highly important to me. But, you may find that after reviewing after a day or two that something doesn't seem right with this expectation. I will reiterate that there is power in the written word, especially if those words are your own. Your list of expectations may change somewhat because you've had time to rest your mind from thinking about the expectations, but now you are able to see exactly how you think. You may come to the conclusion that this expectation is not realistic. Therefore, there is no action required to fulfill an expectation that is unrealistic. However, you will find that additional tasks and resources are required to change your thought pattern in regards to the expectation because the actual expectation came from a specific state of mind. Unless attempts are made to change that particular state of mind then the expectation will live in your subconscious mind longer than you expect.

This realization does not occur overnight so that's why it is important to revisit this worksheet until you are confident that your expectations are realistic as possible before moving towards the fulfillment of those expectations. It may also be very beneficial to let someone you trust review the list as well. The person you trust with reviewing this list should also have your best interest at heart as well because. This will help to reassure you that the best of intentions are being employed in your favor. Allowing the additional perspective will more than likely provide an outlook that you have yet to consider and can provide more clarity as to why your expectations are as such.

Forming healthy and realistic expectations is very important in regards to how they are manifested upon other people. I mentioned before that people with certain roles in our lives come with specific expectations. A sister and a wife carry totally different expectations whereby a sister can love you unconditionally but a wife's love comes with specific conditions attached. A mate is meant to compliment you in areas where it is needed while bringing a sense of fulfillment that is derived from physical and emotional attraction. A friend or associate also come with predetermined expectations but those expectations must be as realistic as possible and agreed upon in some way. Many times we tend to create expectations that the other person is unaware of and when these expectations are not met we want to blame the other person. The truth is that if your value system is different than someone else's then your mutual expectations may be different and will require some definition.

Take a look at the expectations you've listed that are associated with other people. After taking some time away from the list do you see any expectations that now seem unhealthy or realistic? Sometimes, we have no idea the amount of pressure we place on others when we expect them to meet expectations that seem too burdensome or sometimes impossible to meet. The members of my past relationships were living up to my vision of what I thought a relationship was supposed to be. I felt the need to be rescued and led as if somehow hoping that they would fill the role of my father and my grandmother. It wasn't their responsibility to rescue me. It was my responsibility to save myself before deciding to become involved with these people. The same goes for friendships. I was the friend that needed everyone else but did not feel that I could provide the same benefit in return. Basically, I was so busy thinking about what others needed to do for me to feel safe that I forgot that I also should work on becoming a contributing party to their lives as well.

Pretty soon, unrealistic expectations can lead to resentment from all parties involved, heightened frustration, and probably emotionally destructive results. One hint is that if you feel that an expectation is at all unrealistic then more than likely it is. How did you feel when you felt as though an unrealistic expectation was pushed upon you? My experiences included feelings of confusion, disbelief at times, and the inability to see the benefit of my association with that person. These are common feelings when we place unrealistic expectations upon others and part of the purpose for doing the exercise was to allow you to recognize where the work needs to begin in terms of eliminating unrealistic expectations.

Another major issue regarding expectations is the process whereby we relay those expectations to others. Often times, in any type of relationship, we mistakenly assume that all parties involved are well aware of what is expected of them. Let's use an employer and employee as our first example. Usually, when a position is posted it lists a set of qualifiers that are used to weed out what is considered either over qualified or under qualified applicants. They may expect an application to have an undergraduate degree in a particular area of study, at least five years of continuous experience, and the flexibility to travel when needed. These are all expectations that were presented at the beginning of the process. Then, prospects are selected from a pool of applicants based on the information provided as application for the position. Usually, the prospects are interviewed at least once before a decision is made. Once the position is filled the new application is provided a job description. This description outlines the expectations for his or her position. Once these expectations have been relayed to you it is up to you to meet or exceed those expectations. If you meet or exceed the expectations you may receive an award of some kind but if you do not meet the expectations then you will probably be reprimanded in some way.

This concept can be applied to interpersonal relationships as well. The reason why it is so important to relay expectations as soon as possible is because you are then providing the other party an opportunity to state whether or not they can meet a particular expectation and whether or not he or she believes it is realistic or not. In addition, you are setting the stage for dialog that is necessary at the beginning of any type of relationship, especially romantic relationships. Your expectations are a reflection of what you desire and are selfish in nature because you are only thinking about what is required of others to make you feel happy, fulfilled, or otherwise relevant in a relationship. Keeping that in mind, it is best to begin the exploration of expectations as early as possible. The conversation should not focus on how a certain individual should strive to meet your expectations but instead focus on the expectations of a certain role. For example, we usually have the same set of expectations for a boyfriend or girlfriend and they aren't usually tied to a specific person. This makes the conversation regarding expectations less targeted and provides for a conversation that is conducive to setting guidelines as to how the relationship is going to be conducted and if particular expectations can be met. From that point you can decide whether or not to continue the activities that are necessary to strengthen the relationship.

Initially, expectations are all about "I." In this regard, it is usually very difficult to begin the "we" part of the relationship until the "I" part is established. Simply put, it is difficult to create a sense of togetherness without understanding what each party needs to feel appreciated and for the union, regardless of the basis of the union, to feel productive and moving in a direction that all parties feel is positive. It is perfectly alright to be selfish in the beginning in terms of stating what you need in order to feel that the relationship has a chance of being viable because there is minimal emotional investment thus far.

This is why it is preferable to have these conversations BEFORE deciding to commit to a particular type of relationship because we tend to sometimes lose focus and make decisions based on emotional responses that act as filters to what should be a more rational set of decisions. It is also preferable to have such conversations in a relaxed and controlled environment because expectations are very important and the relaying of this information must not suffer from outside interference. This can be done at a scheduled time when all parties are mentally free and more receptive to active listening and absorption of the details. If you feel you are unable to talk freely and openly at that time then I would advise you to reschedule the conversation for a date and time that is soon after the initial scheduled time. Also, the conversation can be worked in during times of joyous interaction where the mood is light and optimistic. Remember that you must also be receptive to the other person's expectations as well because relationships should be viewed as mutually beneficial. Ask yourself if you can meet the expectations presented to you from someone else. If the answer is no then it is less difficult to sever ties, if necessary. On the other hand, what may seem like far reaching expectations may have actually come at a perfect time because you may be in need of personal expansion that has otherwise not been required up to this point in your life.

    Some people can only do as much as they've ever experienced while others are more capable of providing more based on the fact that they can emulate what they hope to achieve in the future. For example, two employees performing the same tasks may operate in different ways. Employee number one follows his job description to the letter and performs usually higher than average. Employee number two also follows her job description to the letter but also volunteers to take on other tasks and seizes additional opportunities at every turn. Employee number one isn't doing anything wrong at all but he is simply doing what he is accustomed to doing, which he does quite well. Employee number two may be focused on the goal of getting into a management position over that same department so she is capable of stretching her arms just a little more in order to get to the prize. Employee number one will probably catch up sooner or later but because he is focused at being great at THAT particular job he will more than likely stay in that position much longer.

Both scenarios encompass positive attributes, but the difference is that the current manager of the department may begin to rely on employee number two to take on additional tasks because she has set the expectation as such. The same is true for romantic relationships. We may speak about our expectations and our desires but the mark is usually set by our actions. So, it is wise to only agree to expectations that you feel you can live up to and to also accept people in roles that you honestly feel that they will fulfill. We've all been there before including me. I had to learn to not make promises based on the person I hope to become but to accept what I am capable of doing at this point in time. There is no doubt that you will change as time progresses but there is no guarantee as to just how much and how soon it will transpire into something noticeable to others.

Expectations are used to create the unit of measurement by which all types of relationships are measured, even if the relationship is the one that you learn to have with yourself. Once the expectations are relayed it is then much easier to hold others accountable. Reminders are sometimes necessary because certain things are forgotten as a natural part of life. If done correctly, the expectations will gradually transfer from being all about each individual's set of expectations to expectations that can be achieved when working together. Also, expectations can also be used to make sure that you hold yourself accountable for the agreements that you've made to yourself in terms of what you hope to achieve, how you achieve your goals, and the feelings associated with those achievements.

CHAPTER 10
THE PURGE: CREATING ROOM FOR POSITIVE CHANGE

> ***Personal Pledge:*** *In order to welcome positive change I must also welcome the pain that accompanies the separation and departing of what and whom no longer works in my favor of my personal advancement. It is only then that I will be able to fully welcome and enjoy the unfamiliar, yet beneficial, fruit that shall hang from my continuously-growing tree.*

Any prospect of change presents unfamiliar territory. Along with unfamiliarity, change may also be accompanied by pain, loss, excitement, as well as confusion. These emotional attributes lend to the reason why some of us find it difficult to move forward with positive change. It is easier to sit in a space of comfort because we find an odd peace when we know what to expect and having learned to roll with the punches per each situation. I, along with countless others, can attest to this fact wholeheartedly. There were times that I reneged on the promises I made to myself to welcome positive change. I feared the unknown that an optimistic yet unguaranteed future had in store for me. As a result I reverted back to what I was used to doing, although unhappy with the same results, simply because it was comfortable and predictable. I'd repeat the cycle of becoming frustrated with myself, committing to change, then undoing the commitment in order to return to a place of comfort. The old habits that kept me bound within my own disappointment were often celebrated then despised then celebrated again. At some point I began to resent myself too much to continue the vicious cycle of crippling comfort and I had to ask myself "why am I so frightened to welcome what has always been waiting for me"?

Before I learned to accept all that came with change I had to face some hard realizations about my fears and why I'd rather remain immobile. I realized that I was afraid to allow the required death of certain parts of my existence to take place. Like a tree that must lose its leaves from a prior season in order to make room for new growth, I too had to allow the separation of what did not or no longer worked in my favor in order to make room for what just might work. I had to decide at some point that I was going to either forcefully detach the dead weight or let it fall by the wayside by its own doing. The uselessness of dead weight was slowing my progress to a screeching halt. My spirit was suffering as I repeatedly created false justifications that allowed me to continue to tote around my burden. The more I carried it, the lower my esteem fell, until the ground level became the most familiar place on earth. If I could've sank further I would have. Although I was not yet prepared, I knew that the only way to grow was to forcibly remove whatever stood in the way of my personal growth. I had to surrender to the power of the purge.

One of the hardest lessons I had to learn was that the purge would happen automatically without warning and that I was not in total control of the process. Also, I had to accept that although the process would be highly uncomfortable it was indeed purposeful. To deny myself the opportunity to go through the process would be the same as denying myself the right to grow and expand. The portion of the process that proved most difficult for me to accept was the separation and loss of people; some I've known for the better parts of my life and some I've only known for a short period of time. This subset also included specific family members. Who would ever think that members of one's own family would be included in this group? It is a phenomenon that most of us will never be prepared for because family is SUPPOSED TO BE in your corner; or so we often assume. But again, it is necessary.

Up to this point I've touched upon topics related to the importance of owning your truth, the power and benefits of forgiveness and the renewal/replenishment of self-love. These acts promote and sponsor your readiness to accept the challenges that positive change will present because you will learn to stand in your own way less often while listening and acting upon opportunities that serve your best interests. Also, your probability of learning and accepting the valuable lessons embedded within each hardship has now increased because you accept that every experience a WORTHWHILE experience regardless of the initial outcome. You also accept the fact that every change begins with your choice to move towards it. You've also gone as far as to visualize yourself within the picture of success. That once-lofty goal doesn't seem as far-fetched as it did when you first envisioned it. But nothing prepares you for "The Purge" because the pain cannot be prevented and it is sneaky yet highly calculated. You will not understand the benefit of the process until you accept it.

I describe the purge as the necessary removal of debris that has accumulated as a direct result of personal advancement. We are all familiar with the term "debris". This term is generally used to describe trash or remnants of something that has been destroyed or otherwise undone. In order to become better for yourself you must do away with anything and everything that now serves as garbage in your life. You didn't notice the debris before because it was on par with how you felt about yourself at the time. In fact, it was the debris that helped to support your lowly view of yourself. It was the company to your misery and just like most garbage; it reeked of despair and abandon. Now you are able to see the debris for what it really is; which is a complete and total hindrance that trips you up at every pass. Not only was it a hindrance, but the sight of it continuously perpetuated the negatively skewed vision that you had of your own future. As you continue to become better for yourself you will be able to distinguish the refuse from the treasures that are worth keeping and honoring.

Whenever you decide to enact any type of personal change it directly affects some or everyone that is attached to you. Aside from family, mostly everyone else is attached to you based on the version of yourself that is presented at certain points of your life. In other words, the friends and associates that you've formed bonds with are directly related to the esteem that you feel for yourself. We usually believe that it is merely based on commonalities such as viewpoints on sports and political issues or the enjoyment of certain hobbies. That's not the case at all. We run into many others that may share some of the same philosophies but that acknowledgment doesn't usually result in an instant connection.

On a subconscious level we tend to gravitate towards others whose self-esteem are a match to our own or somewhat lower. For example, a person with extremely low self-esteem would feel highly uncomfortable, or even intimidated, of someone who has a higher esteem or regard for themselves. This is usually because the lower the esteem, the more self-conscious and self-reflecting one's outlook becomes. The higher esteemed individual will exhibit actions of pride and contentment that may come of cocky and slightly arrogant to those that are unable to manifest similar actions. This is why the individual with lower self-esteem may attract a person with a higher sense of self-value as well as purpose but may not be willing or able to nurture a healthy bond with that same individual. Keeping that in mind, I want you to think about everyone that is in your immediate social circle. They are a part of your circle because on some level you find comfort in their presence. You may have moments of comparison but it does not create such an uncomfortable environment that results in your desire to flee or detach. The relationship stays intact so long as you feel comfortable and safe (emotionally and physically). This does not mean that your connections are all great connections. It just means that you are connected by some common attributes or actions that prevent either party from making the other feel uncomfortable or heavily judged.

Each step that you commit towards self-improvement helps to create a new iteration of your entire being. You and others will notice the shift in your personality which includes your body language and the language you use to describe yourself and your aspirations. You may also start to smile more often, speak more encouragingly about yourself and others, adopt a firmer handshake, and even walk more upright than before. In addition, you may also start to dress and speak the part of your future self as you prepare to walk into your rightful space of achievement. But as you proceed to move upward, you will begin to notice the shaking of your branches and that some of the leaves that once provided coverage are on the verge of falling away. What does fall away will make room for newer and healthier growth to occur.

Are you ready to separate from the people that either allowed or helped to foster the lowly view you have of yourself? At the very worst this can include friends whom you felt were dear to you as well as family members you may have felt a special connection with. But what if the connection to specific people was sponsored by misery, self-loathing, depression, and hatred towards the condition of your life during a specific time period? At some point you will come to realize that one of the only reasons why some of them remained connected to you was because the view of your misery made their own level of misery and despair look a little better. You were in a place that did not allow you to judge them. Let's face it. One miserable person can't judge another, right? So unbeknownst to you, most of your circle may consist of miserable people who felt most comfortable around another miserable person. This isn't the case for everyone because positive change can also come as a result of previous positive changes and represent an upward movement from an already positive place. In any case, any future positive change will require a purge to happen. You will trade what doesn't work for what may work. The rewards for your hard work will also be bestowed as the purge process takes place so do not feel surprised if the rewards seem bittersweet considering the cost that you were required to pay.

One of the most painful examples of the purge process happened during a time when I was about to begin my journey into manhood and allow my adult dreams to set sail. I had to decide to either continue to allow myself to be continuously victimized or decide to do away with the conduit of my victimization. My education was my salvation throughout my childhood and teenage years because it allowed me to escape to a place where I felt superior as opposed to the various situations that negatively impacted my childhood. So, it was quite natural for me to consider going to college upon finishing high school. During the last week of my senior year in high school I landed a job at a local fast food restaurant. I had worked for three days. That was until I burned my arm on the hamburger grill. At that moment I convinced myself that there had to be something much better out there waiting for me. So, I firmly decided that I was going to attend college and began applying for admission to schools in Texas. Within a matter of a couple of weeks I got accepted, quit my job, and told my family I was moving back to Houston to continue my education. Mostly, everyone was optimistic about my prospects. Then, came the moment when I had to tell my father about my decision. It wasn't as if he was ever engaged in my education but I felt I owed him the courtesy of telling him that I was moving in pursuit of a better life than rural Louisiana had to offer me. I explained to him that I quit my local fast food job to pursue my education. I also told him that I planned to pursue a Bachelor's of Science degree in Business Administration. Actually, I told him that I wanted to pursue a "B.S. degree". His response began with disarming body language. He paused for a moment then looked at me with resentment in his eyes. I instantly realized that whatever was to come out of his mouth at that point would immediately crush my soul. He then says to me "you're going to quit a job you just started to go to some college? B.S. to me means bullshit. I should take your computer and crush it in the middle of the street". His words caused my body to tense up so much that you could have knocked me over with a feather and I would have fallen and shattered into a billion emotional pieces. The mere mention of trashing my computer enraged me because he knew that my computer was the bridge to my escape. My writing was one of the only joys that allowed me to escape my cyclic mental hell. To also ask me why I'd quit a fast food job just to attend college further cemented my opinion that he either didn't see a bountiful future for me or that his own self-hatred could not allow someone else, even if it's his own child, to excel in areas that he chose not to. It was one of the biggest hurts to land on my heart through his words. It felt like parental betrayal; as if he had somehow reneged on his duties and promises that any parent should swear by.

For the first time that I can recall I was forced to make a decision that would benefit me while foregoing all the spiritual agreements I was told to keep intact. The Holy Bible commanded me to honor thy father and mother so that my days would be long. But how could I honor my father who CHOSE to cause his first born emotional pain repeatedly and heavily? At the age of seventeen I decided that the need for a healthier well-being far outweighed the toxic connection that I had with my father. After my spirit absorbed his words I simply turned and walked away. From that moment I decided to never share another positive or monumental thought or life event with him ever again. It hurt beyond measure that my own father could not find the strength to set aside his own personal demons to give encouragement to his oldest child to dream big or to simply take a chance. That single event, and the decision to exclude him from that facet of my life, negatively altered the way I spoke of my aspirations to others. In the end I decided to purge what wasn't working in my favor. Although painful, I accepted the fact that the process was necessary.

The testimony I shared was used specifically to emphasize the fact that anytime you decide to purge someone or something, such as a bad habit or action that negatively impacts your own personal progress, you should first expect some type of anxiety or distress surrounding the decision to either purge or push through. The anxiety is rooted in the fact that you must decide when and how to part ways if it becomes necessary. It can be either through a gradual decrease in communication or completely cold-turkey, depending on how quickly you feel that the purge needs to happen. In an emotionally distressful situation it may be necessary to just let go and deal with the pain of it all later. In other situations it might be easier to slowly transform the relationship into something that does work such as a mere association that doesn't come with the expectation of a certain level of support.

One whose energy works for you will embrace your changes and will gladly welcome the role of supporter without being provoked. You won't have to explicitly request their backing. In fact, one in this position will more than likely come to you and ask you what is required of them to support you. One whose energy works against you will find themselves constantly questioning your motivation, planting small seeds of discouragement, and/or trying to convince you to continue the bad habits that kept you at an esteem level that were comfortable with. For example, if your goal is to lose weight you will find it harder to succeed if a family member or friend is constantly sabotaging your efforts with such acts as offering you food that is counterproductive to your goal or a family member that tries to discourage your desire/need to exercise even if the goal ultimately helps to save your life. You should never have to wonder whether or not someone is standing behind you and supporting you or working against you even when it is obvious that your change may positively affect your life. It is a completely unnecessary stress that will hurt, harm, and hinder you at every turn.

There is also a part of the purge process that is completely out of your control and will prove to the most painful version of the entire process; when people choose to part with you before you decide to part with them. Most of us have experienced this in some form but were unable to understand why it had to happen. When you begin to make positive and noticeable strides in your personal well-being everyone notices but everyone does not respond in the same way; especially if your misery or self-doubt seemingly elevated someone else's self-worth when compared to yours. It begins with subtly communication changes such as frequency in dialog and the difference in the types of exchanges that usually occurred. There is also a noticeable change in body language that either says "I welcome, accept, and support your change" or "I'm intimidated and uncomfortable with your level of confidence". As you climb the ladder of personal success you will be met with both well-deserved cheers and unwarranted jeers. Comments such as "you've changed" or "you think you're all that" may be received more often than you had anticipated. At first listen, you may question yourself and wonder if you've become this self-centered and self-serving person that you are somehow made out to be. But I suggest that you first question the messenger. How does your self-esteem at this moment in time compare to theirs? Is your personal elevation forcing them to take notice of their own place in the world around them? Also, is your decrease in misery resulting in less company for them? If you've made no outward gestures, either physically or verbally, that would seemingly diminish their esteem then I would chalk it up to their own insecurities resulting in intimidation. Instead of accepting intimidation it is skewed and portrayed as a negative action that is coming from you as if to look down upon them. The accusation can hurt especially if you are knowingly doing everything in your power not to cast a negative light on anyone else as you move up the ladder of personal improvement.

Have you begun to notice that some of your friends or associates no longer call you to invite you to hang out or that you are finding out about events after they have occurred? The well-wishes and check-ins have become less frequent and the usually effervescent run-ins in public have been replaced with a sideways extended handshake and emotionless hug? The smile that you once expected on the other end of the greeting becomes less personal and more generic. It's the same casual types of greetings you've noticed them give to associates that they really had no personal connection to. Now, you are slowly becoming that same type of associate; the one that they no longer check on or feel personally invested in. It is indeed painful because I'm sure that there were no notations in your personal improvement plan that included being dumped for becoming better for yourself. It may even cause you to want to question certain individuals as this is happening. If so, you should prepare yourself for a truth that may not be what you expect to hear.

One way to look at the purge process is related to the spirit of discernment that God provides as a means of protection and filtering. Discernment takes into consideration everything that God has planned for your life compared to everything that is currently encompassing your life. It is a higher level of judgment that does not take into consideration hate, bitterness, or extreme cynicism. Its acceptance forces you to set aside the tunnel vision created as a result of your life experiences and allow what God sees as beneficial to impact your life. The gift of discernment does not always come naturally because we desire to control every outcome even when 95% of the moving parts are not even under our control. Discernment is a clear act of faith and trust and it allows you to cast away your fears, intimidation, and control and say "God, who and what is it that you have for me". He is then able to slowly show you what is good for you even if you may not fully comprehend the who's, what's, where's, why's and how's. But, the convergence of all that is good for you will make eventually make sense as part of the grand scheme for your success.

One of my dearest friends, named Henry for the sake of this example, called me and asked me to meet him for drinks because he really needed to talk. I immediately became worried because the tone in which he expressed his request was very different from his usual tone of voice. After my usual visitation with my kids I met with him at one of my favorite restaurants. As to eliminate my feeling of suspense I immediately asked that he tell me exactly what was going on. He divulged to me that he had begun to make preparations to go back to college to complete the undergraduate degree that he had abandoned years prior. He believed that his career would greatly benefit from the distinction and had finally built up the courage to try again. Then with his head hung low and dropping eye contact, he stated that he felt that some of his friends and family were attempting to. As an example, he stated that one of his dearest friends asked him why would he want to go back to school and also asked if he was sure he wanted to give up hanging out on most weekends since the classes would be conducted on the weekends. He also stated that some of his family members seemed to question his ability to succeed in an area that he had previously abandoned. Henry was on the verge of crying. I knew it was my time to interject and to help him understand what he was going through.

I asked Henry "how much pain are you willing to accept in exchange for happiness?" He was confused by the mention of pain but I was very absolute in my question. I explained to him that almost everything that is done in anticipation of receipt of happiness, joy, and peace of mind comes with a cost that most are not willing to even consider. I further explained that this cost includes the loss of attachments that he had grown accustomed to fostering. I also explained that although he may not yet want to believe it, some people within his immediate circle may become envious of his desire to succeed and will subsequently attempt to either sabotage or stall his efforts to succeed but that he should not take it personal because it is no reflection of him but how they ultimately feel about themselves as compared to him. However, each step he takes toward his goal will increase his self-esteem. His heightened self-esteem will be received by some as a light that will seemingly cast a shadow upon their own insecurities. I also stated that his friends and family will attempt to deflect their insecurities upon him and attempt to make him believe that he has tried to outshine them.

As I had previously explained to him the purge process will prune everything that has become deadweight. The space that was once allotted for the deadweight is now free to be occupied by the new people and things that his courage, determination, and hard work will attract. As he begins to climb the ladder of personal success he will slowly begin to experience gains on both a personal and professional level. The people that he will begin to attract will be more like-minded, less intimidated, and naturally encouraging. Those that survive the purge process will already embody these characteristics without having been asked. I also explained that the way he navigates the world will slowly change as it relates to his body language and the way he speaks of himself. Finally I stated that he will begin to command more respect while still being able to offer the same amount of respect and encouragement to others in similar situations.

It took him a moment to understand everything that I had mentioned. After a while of conversation I once again asked him how much loss, and quite possibly pain, he was willing to endure in order to succeed. I also asked if he was ready to walk towards the bounty that God already promised as a result of his faith and hard work. Then, I reminded him that God stands in between him and those that mean him harm and acts as the agent that separates the oil from his water, so that his calm waters can rest atop of the contamination that will be encountered at every turn. Finally, I told him that his progress will intimidate anyone in his circle that remains stagnant within their own progress and that their hope may be to siphon the fuel that moves him forward in order to hold him back for their own benefit. In turn, everything that they do towards you is a direct reflection of how they feel about themselves. Afterwards I noticed that his head was no longer hung low and that he appeared to be more energized. He stated that although he was afraid of the purge process, he understood that it was necessary. In the end he came to the decision to accept the procedure as it happened.

The sooner we accept the pain and confusion that results from the purge, the faster we are able to confidently follow through with the work required to move towards the next level of success. In fact, the fear of the purge process is what sometimes influences one's fear of success. We are afraid to be seen as intimidating or to be negatively influenced by those that actually meant us harm in the first place. Also, we are sometimes afraid to be told that we have changed for fear of becoming an outcast. However, as I mentioned previously, the empty spaces resulting from the purge process will eventually be filled with more substantial elements that will make sense sooner than later. The choices required to improve your quality of life far outweighs the chance of being continuously discouraged in order to save relationships that no longer fit within your life. Progress evokes changes, just as a lack of progress does not. In the end, the choice has always been yours to make. Sometimes we have to live on the frightening side of change before we are able to accept the pleasures and bounty of our work.

GOD*credible*
Pronounced [God-kred-uh-buh l]

Adjective
1. Spiritually qualified, eligible, and deserving
2. Irrevocable supernatural validation.
3. Far more superior than incredible.
4. YOU

CHAPTER 11

SELF-MARKETING 101

> ***Personal Pledge:*** *I will come to understand the importance of putting my best foot forward while remaining honest about who I really am and the work that is left to do to get what and where I feel I belong. My levels of self-respect, respect for others, confidence, and determination are always portrayed through my outward actions therefore perceivable by others.*

You've taken all of the time required to get yourself prepared to go after, as well as to receive, everything that you feel you are worthy of having. You've even expelled most of the habits that prove to be disastrous while managing the ones that are a permanent fixture of the fabric of your being. You've also continued your personal development by eliminating most of your wasteful and negative thinking, and slowly began to strengthen your incredible support system. Everything seems to be in order until you realize that now you have to present your persona and agenda unto the world in order to attain the resources you need to reach your goals. Your presentation is going to be viewed by everyone and you should hold the belief that you are being judged by each foot that you choose to put forward.

First impressions are always the most memorable impressions because they truly set the tone for any other type of future interaction and they are usually hard to reverse or change. We can make some people feel comfortable, uncomfortable, eager to know more, or eager to leave our presence. We are quick to form opinions of others based on appearance, gestures, mannerisms, and interactions with others in our immediate area. It is usually hard to change such an opinion once it is made. Take for instance your application for a particular job. While the requirements include the construction of a resume that outlines your education and qualifications it is usually left to you to format the resume to the best of your abilities. Since your resume is the first point of communication between you and the employer they must base your qualifications on that same resume and a cover letter. These documents are used is qualifiers as they sort through the myriad of other resumes and cover letters.

What you may not realize is that your inability to land that job may have had nothing to do with your skills or qualifications. It may, however, have everything to do with the presentation of those skills and qualifications. The same is true for how we present ourselves to the world. You've taken the time to do what was necessary to build up your self-esteem and you understand what it is that you want from this life that you live and now is the time to command the respect and positive attention in not-so-obvious ways. One thing I must mention is that this is not about portraying anything that isn't true to who you are. It is about bringing forth your best qualities as precursors to getting to know who you are. Let's face it, we all have issues and habits that some will view as intolerable or negative but if we continue to allow the seemingly negative traits to outshine our positive aspects we end up becoming our own worst enemy all over again.

A handshake, eye contact, mode of speaking, the way you walk, style of dress, your responses to questions and your body language are all contributing factors to how people perceive you. Think of yourself as a walking billboard that onlookers are able to review for only a few seconds. What would you want your billboard to reveal about you in that limited amount of time? Remember that spectators only have a few seconds to take in everything that is being presented to them. Afterwards, they form an opinion as to whether or not an additional inquiry is required. You've seen billboards that inspired you to go home and do research on a particular company or product and you've also seen billboards that leave a sour taste in your mouth based on the content, the message, or a combination of both. Our focus should lie in the creation of a truthful, positive, and consistent expression of who we are while drawing to us those things that we desire or positions that we aspire to reach.

The concept of becoming a walking billboard can be applied to nearly every facet of our lives. For years I wondered why I seemed to attract only attract particular types of people into my personal space. Usually, that person would end up inflicting some type of pain in my life, whether I provoked it or not. It was almost always in the form of manipulation or using my painful past against me. Then, as usual, I would question myself as to how this could have happened again. I never thought of asking myself how to make myself more accountable for what I was attracting.

A few years ago I read a passage from a book that stated something about how we can learn to attract what we want. Then, it hit me. I was so concerned about the people I met as opposed to why they were actually attracted to me. Something within my spirit drew their energy to mine. Once I came to this realization I could no longer say that I had no idea why I was a part of a particular entanglement. I had yet gotten to a point where my personal insecurities were undetectable and my painful situations were unobservable. It was as if they could detect my sense of loneliness and desperation without me having to mention a word. My billboard spoke volumes, but in a negative way. I was also attracting exactly what my energy dictated and I provided a glimpse of my desire to feel a sense of completion that I felt could only be provided by another individual and that I felt invaluable otherwise. I believe that I also gave the impression that that person would become my lifeline and that I would forsake all of my loved ones once their place in my world was established. That was all that was needed to attract the usual suspects that I would eventually have to let go. I could not change my billboard until I changed the mechanisms that controlled what my billboard portrayed. This could only happen once I recognized my truth and began to practice the recognition of my issues and forgiveness for those things that were out of my control.

    I'm pretty sure you are now thinking about your own relationship billboard. I feel it is important that we all take into consideration what we present to that person that we hope to have some type of interaction with, whether it is on a platonic level or not. By evaluating your current relationship billboard you are allowing yourself the opportunity to effectively analyze the current state of your billboard while recognizing areas of improvement. One of the downfalls of going about this process on our own is that some of us have a skewed view of what we present to others. The next exercise I am going to explain will probably be the most difficult to do because you will be forced to listen to or read the opinions of others as it relates to their opinion of who you are. Some of the answers may be in line with what you already believe to be true while others may shock and even hurt your feelings. Realize that the end goal is to find a common ground of understanding in terms of how and why people form particular opinions about you. Listening to their opinions does not necessarily mean that their opinions are true. It just means that you are open to the honesty of an opinion outside of your own. I usually suggest using at least three people who are not closely bonded to your spirit because we want to not let feelings and sympathy get in the way of valuable and authentic opinions.

    You may wonder how the billboard concept applies to the rest of our aspirations in life. In most cases it serves as the starting point of projecting the energy that will attract what we desire. When coaching individuals regarding relationships I usually tell them that people of a certain level of awareness and acceptance will only find successful partnership with other individuals that possess at least the same level of those same attributes. This does not mean that the person is without fault or in need of further repair. This simply means that the person is willing to be more accountable without being provoked to do so. As a result, compromise will come much easier and the realizations that more work needs to be done will originate with the person who needs it. Also, their level of compassion increases because they already know what they bring to the table and how this can affect the other person. In other words, they are more apt to consider the feelings of the other person.

Now, try applying the billboard concept to areas such as your career or social networking. How can you maximize your potential for positive impact? What can you do to make your presence more pleasantly memorable? You want to develop a brief personal presentation that speaks to who you are today while leaving the past exactly where it should be. If you feel more confident about yourself it is your responsibility to show it in your stride and by displaying a more upright posture when walking or approaching new people. Trust me, it speaks to our subconscious level of perception and serves as part of your signature in the minds of the receiver. It is time to understand that a little either goes a very long way or falls drastically short of the intended goal.

The easiest way to start to positively alter your billboard is by learning the power of body language. Giving a firm hand shake reaffirms to others that you believe in your physical presence and that the oral presentation that may follow will provide additional notice to your confidence in what you believe as well as what you hope to gain from the meeting. You will also create a sense of assurance in the ideas that you will possibly present while showing a keen interest in the information that will be shared by other parties who are privy to the conversation. Adding a smile to that handshake shows a genuine comfort and security with yourself and that you are willing to approach situations with an optimistic attitude while looking for ways to create a positive opportunity. Standing as upright as possible affects not only how people view your presence but it also affects how you feel about yourself. Walking around with your head down gives the impression that you purposely avoid personal engagement and may lead to the opinion that you are unapproachable. Making eye contact with someone, even for a mere second, can give the impression that you are interested and that you are paying attention. This is especially important in the midst of conversation. A great deal of learning can be gathered through insightful conversation or nonchalant banter. These simple gestures tell the world that you are present and accountable and that you appreciate yourself enough to worry about how you affect others. If I met you I would hope to be able to respect your billboard. I may not grow to like you or create a space for you in my world but I hope to be able to respect the authority of your life.

Sometimes we are unaware of just how powerful our subconscious mind works when creating assumptions about people and things. The billboard approach focuses on affecting the subconscious mind of your observers and it creates a long-lasting impression that almost always influences the conscious parts of our thinking. The priority is to learn to project your positive attributes while portraying a sense of peace of mind and a high level of self-satisfaction. That's why it is best to attract people and things to who you have become today as opposed to creating an illusion wrapped around what you hope to become tomorrow. Be the best person you can at this very moment in time while understanding that goals for tomorrow do exist but that the time is not guaranteed. When we learn to not take time for granted we will begin to enjoy the current day while harboring great anticipation for what may come. Always continue to strive for improvement because growing and learning ceases only when you decide that it does. As you become more knowledgeable your billboard will become bigger because of the positive enhancements. There will be more for others to ingest as well as a growing desire to learn what they've yet to discover. Your goal is get others to take notice of your presence in a positive way without forcing it. Remember, you never know who is actively paying attention to what you may have to offer towards a worthwhile opportunity.

Intermission IV: I AM

I AM...

The sum of my inherited parts yet free to create new cycles

Fearfully and wonderfully created

The little boy you touched inappropriately that evolved into a forgiving and trusting soul

The man who once felt his voice brought shame that now speaks to the masses with conviction and confidence

The first-born child of a broken man that refuses to let his brokenness deem him any less complete yet open to new well-fitting "pieces"

Fearless

Humble

Focused

Trusting

Compassionate

Deserving

Worthy

Forgiving

Proud

Afraid, but willing to try

I AM...COMPLETE in spite of my IMPERFECTIONS

The "*I AM*" statement is one of the most powerful phrases known to man no matter the language in which it is spoken. It's that MIND-OVER-MATTER type of statement that can command strength in areas where you once believed you were weak and unstable. On the flipside it can also bring a grown man to his knees if he succumbs to the negative connotations that can so easily be attached to it. The power wielded by what we believe about ourselves is very monumental in that it can either help us turn the tides in overcoming low self-esteem, a negative self-image, and other dangerous outlooks that can persuade us to further harm ourselves to a possible point of disrepair.

The *I Am* phrase by itself dictates that what follows this declaration is what is to eventually become of the person that creates it and believes it. For example, if I continually say to myself "*I am a failure*" I will surely behave in ways that live up to such a strong yet negative declaration about myself. It will become evident in the energy I exude towards the goals that I so dearly want to accomplish because I will begin behaving as a defeatist or one who surrenders easily at the first sight of trouble. It will also begin to show up in how I deal with and treat others. My internal emotional motor will never reach full power because I have already predicted a terrible outcome. When failure is the prediction then it provides little reason to put forth one's best effort to act and achieve at the highest level. Also, the moments of success that are sure to come will be outweighed by the moments of failure even if the successful experiences actually outnumber the failures that are having the biggest impact on your esteem. This is only one example of how the *I Am* statement can have negative weight and pull one below a safe personal baseline as it relates to personal and professional achievement. This type of connotation, along with other negative variations, usually becomes very difficult to overcome or turn around after an extended period of time. For some it may have begun as early as childhood and continued through adolescence all the way up to and through adulthood. The programming was set in motion so long ago that any other way of thinking may seem virtually impossible. But the truth is that it is never too late to empower yourself and reprogram your way of thinking in a way that will direct your behavior in the positive direction. If you can convince your mind that you are fully capable and deserving then you've achieved one of the greatest milestones towards self-empowerment.

Are you ready to positively identify who you completely are to yourself first and then to the rest of us? Are you ready to take one of the easiest yet most fearless steps to begin to reprogram the way you view yourself without including type of external comparisons? Only you can supply the words that support your *I Am* statement. Once you are able to perceive your strengths and deservedness you are then capable of reprogramming the negative thoughts related to your functionality as a deserving human being one statement at a time. Putting all issues aside you are already capable of fulfilling all of your desires. One of the most interesting things that will happen is that even if you do not believe a single word about your positive *I Am* statement today you will eventually persuade yourself to believe that everything you said is in fact true and that you deserve the positive inflections you are bestowing upon yourself. Over time your actions and attitude will form around these powerful declarations as you remind yourself during the lowest of times that these statements never have to change if YOU do not allow it.

Now it is time for you to complete your *I Am* statement

Instructions:

1. Fill in as many positive attributes and affirmations about yourself. Also include any future aspirations that Examples include:

    I am a wonderful mother

    I am patient

    I am nurturing

    I am a future doctor

    I am a wonderful confidant

Now, I'd like you to complete your positive *I Am* statement in the blank lines provided below.

I Am

_____

_____

_____

_____

_____

_____

_____

Sit or Stand 2.0

_____

_____

_____

_____

_____

2. Next, commit to repeating your *I Am* statement to yourself at least once per day for an entire week; preferably in the morning and also at night before going to bed.
3. Finally, at week's end, observe the change in your self-perception. Repeat this exercise if necessary.

CHAPTER 12

RECOGNIZING AND BUILDING YOUR SUPPORT SYSTEM

> ***Personal Pledge:*** *Today, I make a promise to myself to begin to recognize what I need in order to fulfill my goals and expectations. I will have trust in my support system and will listen to their advice with an open mind. I will also recognize that I must remove all negative components of my support system and replace them with positive and viable resources.*

I'd like you to take a moment to think about the last time you set out to complete a major goal in your life but may have slightly missed the mark. You knew exactly what was required to reach that milestone and you gave it a hell of a shot but just couldn't get past the clearing. You may have fallen into the same trap that most of us do and that is to become caught up in the illusion that you can do any and everything alone, without any valuable assistance from anyone or anything at all. The truth is that while we can definitely achieve some things alone we are definitely either dependent or codependent upon other resources to achieve almost all of our goals. While some things can be achieved by performing all of the work on our own, there are certain tasks, usually larger endeavors, which require external assistance and ongoing support. Entrepreneurs require clients, doctors require nurses and patients, and students require teachers. It's time to start considering your needs as it relates to reaching and maintaining your goals.

Most successful people require assistance. This assistance can come in the form of coaches, mentors, teachers, assistants, and friends and family who have your best interest at heart. Take some time and think back to your fondest memories during your childhood or teenaged years. Those memories were probably occupied with other people such as a grandparent, parent, cousin, best friend, or even a school mate. The feelings that make up those moments are feelings of security, dedication, obligation, and a kindred interest in your success. There also exited a heightened level of trust that allowed these people to encourage you when you felt incapable of achieving your goals, applauding your success, and holding you to task when they felt that you may have done a disservice to yourself. Without their love and support you may not have had the wherewithal to continue your journey of self-improvement. I've just described the components and the purpose of a healthy support system.

In case you don't understand the definition of support let me attempt to clarify it for you. Dictionary.com defines support as both a verb and noun, but I want to take a moment and work with the verbal definitions for a minute. It means to hold up, sustain, endure, maintain, provide for, uphold, as well as advocate. This means that any element of your support system should be able to perform at least one of these actions. Another thing to note is that your support system does not include only people; it also includes resources that you require to obtain and sustain a healthy state of living. For example, an environment that is conducive to success is vital to your personal success. Also, a strong and healthy belief system can serve as a template for current and future goals by setting the precedent upon which your goals are built and pursued.

Other things, such as education, equipment, and even materials, can serve as your support system if it is serves a role in your positive development.

I am a firm believer in forming connections to things that are familiar and common. As a coach practitioner, I find joy in assisting clients by using familiar imagery as a way to help my clients relate to what can be labeled as a natural approach to understanding the components of a support system. A support system comprises elements that are codependent upon each other in order to create a cohesive and self-sufficient system. When one part of the system falters it usually affects one or more other parts of the system. Also, when one fragment of your system experiences significant growth it usually impacts your entire system in a positive manner. Understanding this correlation allows you to understand the importance of creating the best support system that will assist you in achieving your goals.

I usually use a tree as my example when I discuss the composition of a healthy support system. What comes to mind when you think of a tree? The first thing that comes to my mind are the many variations of types of trees that can be found in nature with each one having a distinct set of characteristics that are distinguishable from every other tree. Some of us think of an entire entity comprised of a trunk, limbs, and leaves that make up a complete organism. Others take the time to make more granular observations as to how every component works together to create the end product. By making granular observations we are able to determine how each small and irregular function is intermingled with another in order to create a successful system. If one of these functions begin to act in an irregular manner it most surely will affect other functions in some way, great or small.

Most trees require a healthy bed of soil as their first defense in growing healthy and robust. As humans, our personal level of achievement is highly affected by the foundation from which our support system is fed. Your foundation, or soil, includes your moral and spiritual beliefs, lessons learned by caregivers such as parents, as well as what you hold near to your heart that controls your most intimate decision making skills. Our foundation is the most substantial component of anyone's support system because it influences every other aspect that we allow to comprise our system. Our judgment of people and relationships is profoundly affected as a direct result of a healthy or unhealthy foundation. For example, my unresolved experiences with abuse resulted in my inability to detect any unhealthy attachments to other people. Therefore, most of my support system was comprised of people and things that fed into my extreme need to feel a sense of belonging that proved to be very unhealthy. I was wreaking havoc on my foundation. Little by little I allowed poisonous actions to seep into my foundation and damage the core of my being. Therefore, anything that continued to spring forth was tainted before it even had a chance to bloom. I would later discover that those connections were in no way part of my support system. If any member of your support system has a negative affect on your foundation then IT IS NOT a part of your support system and must be removed and replaced with a positive counterpart.

This is where embracing your truth plays a large part in strengthening your foundation. When you accept your truth you begin to understand where the cracks and holes exist within your foundation. Every beneficial and unbeneficial element of your foundation is brought to the forefront and now exist points of repair that you would've otherwise been unable to recognize. Once the recognition takes place you are able to understand what it is that you need to fortify those weak spots in your foundation. I once suffered from extreme low self-esteem so every time I allowed someone else to control my value I could feel my foundation growing weaker, as if I truly had no legs to stand on. It became worse if that person left my life because as poisonous as it was, I felt I needed it even though it wasn't beneficial. Anyone's foundation can suffer from wear and tear over time and circumstances but we have the ability to fertilize our foundation with important elements that provide us the emotional and physical nutrients that we need to grow stronger and healthier. Positive nutrients can include such things as encouragement, honesty, and accountability. These three elements provide the wherewithal for you to recognize when encouragement is required and the ability to be honest with yourself by holding yourself accountable for things that you can control and therefore possibly change.

I usually compare the spirit or soul of an individual to that of a tree trunk. The trunk is considered the most vital part of a tree. If the trunk is sick then the ENTIRE tree is Depending on its appearance, one can judge the health of a tree by observing its trunk. The same can be said about your soul. Your actions, reactions, and moods are all manifestations of the health of your soul. By making observations, one can also get a sense of your overall emotional health. What helps to determine the overall health of the trunk of a tree? Its foundation, the types and amount of nutrients received, and the strength of its roots. Your soul is one of the most important parts of your being so it's highly important that we pay attention to what we feed our spirits, both consciously and subconsciously. Dangerous thoughts tend to badger one's spirit in hopes of prevailing. Once the thoughts prevail it is that much easier for other dangerous thoughts and behaviors to take over. At some point it can become so overwhelming that the dangerous thoughts become your reality. Then, every decision and movement that you make is predicated on a bad set of ideals that become harder to reverse over time.

I previously mentioned that the roots are important to the development of a healthy tree. The reason I say this is because the roots serve as the anchor and can prevent a tree from swaying under pressure. The tree now has firm footing to grow straight ahead. In our support system the roots can be compared to the important people in our lives that have made and continue to make great contributions to our spirit. During those dark moments, I failed to remember the people in my life that played an instrumental part in developing my compassion for others and who tried their best to instill a great amount of self-respect, intelligence and sense of self-worth. Those people included my grandparents, my mother, my beloved aunt, and a small group of family members. These people served as my root system even when they had no idea that I spent most of my life suffering in the dark. They had a natural way of uplifting me just enough to not allow me to sink into the darkest of places. I had to learn to extricate anything and anyone that contradicted those feelings. The hardest part of it all was to understand that to lose the negative influences in no way diminished the number of great elements that remained.

Are you fully aware of the people, and their respective contributions, that you have allowed to be a part of your root system?? Is there anyone in your life at the present time that is able to provide the compassion, support, endorsement, honesty and encouragement that you require to flourish internally? If not, can you think of anyone in your past that may have provided that same level of commitment to your personal success such as a parent, family member, dear friend or mentor? If so, then now is the perfect time to find a way to reintroduce them into your life and your growing level of confidence. Your root system can include a hodgepodge of people from both your past and present so long as their contributions are clearly recognizable and functions positively when needed. For a long time all I had to reference were my relationships with my close family members to cling to. Over time I was able to rebuild my trust in people and began to make current connections that directly impacted my root system. New friends who were as equally concerned about my well-being as I was about theirs, business partners and associates, and renewed connections with family members were now part of my root system. I began to flourish at a faster pace and found that my dark moments were shorter in duration because someone was there to recognize them and attempt to pull me out of it. In essence, they tolerated less from me than I did of myself and I could not have been more grateful. Your root system should not only show compassion but also know when and how to hold you accountable for your own progress as well as assisting you in determining those situations that are either out of your league or otherwise unchangeable from your perspective. So, take some time to recognize what it is that you need to flourish and look for those complimentary qualities in others when forming new associations. Therapists and counselors are also great additions to your root system, especially if they are assisting you in your breakthrough and helping you to create positive channels inspiration. Also, by reflecting these qualities upon others you are able to provide support and become a viable member of someone else's root system. The effect can rebound from person to person and you then become a valuable entity to someone else.

Now, we get to the part where some have had a somewhat hard time understanding. We've discussed the foundation, root system, and the trunk of your tree. We haven't mentioned the branches. Nearly every tree has branches that protrude from almost any angle from its trunk. Branches are merely extensions of the trunk; therefore we can view our branches as being extensions of ourselves. Branches are meant to be permanent until a catastrophic event causes severance of the limb or if we notice on our own that the limb is just an unhealthy or dead attachment that must be removed. What comes to mind when you think about your own branches? Think about what you project unto the world and how this affects whatever begins to extend from your spirit. Things that come to mind for myself are bad personal relationships, unfavorable habits, and incomplete goals and dreams. At one point in my life these were my branches. They grew over time and, like branches, caught things that were meant to hit the ground. I was unable to shake away the toxic elements because I felt that everything I came in contact with was worth keeping simply because I was afraid of losing something, whether it was good for me or not. If bad energy was around me I was prone to catching some of it because my branches were conditioned to attracting it. My low self-esteem was the catalyst for the growth of most of these branches. As I sank lower and lower my branches grew longer and stronger, making recovery much more difficult. So, no matter what I decided I didn't want, my branches caught everything that my spirit attracted. The great things fell by the wayside and hit the ground while my branches clung to the items that proved of no benefit to me.

Some of us travel through life not understanding that a great deal of what we have to work through is directly related to what we project unto the world and receive in return. We usually spend more time looking for answers as opposed to paying attention to prevention. You may know why something has happened but do you have any clue as to how to prevent it from happening again? These questions are answered at a deeper level than some of us are willing to explore. By recognizing the toxins in our spirit we come to understand the bottom line of our issues, whether through fault of our own or others. At that point we can expel most of the toxins by instilling small changes to our point of view and our usual habits. As the toxins are released we then begin to notice a change in the chemistry of our own branches. The branches do not die and fall off. Instead we notice a change in the way the branches behave and what the branches begin to attract. No longer are we only attracting negative items. We begin to attract more positive items to add to our inventory necessary for reinvention. The negative items that we attract will lessen and we will have mechanisms in place to deal with the occurrence as it happens. In essence we learn how to control the effects of the negative energy instead of waiting to come from under the darkness. This part of your support system is directly related to your transformation process.

Your branches, and the fruit they bare, are what you present to the world as an extension of your character and are the most noticeable by others. They can be comprised of actual people that exhibit the characteristics of what is good and not so good in your life such as friends that do more harm than good, different relationships that proved disastrous, or anyone associated with dismal points in your life. Branches of these types can be severed either slowly or all-at-once but the decision has to be made as to whether or not these relationships are at all salvageable. If there is room for salvage then recognize the parts of the branch that must be cut back before new and positive growth can begin because once a branch is cut the wrong way it never grows back.

We've moved up from the foundation all the way through to the branches. Now, we get to the leaves of your tree. Leaves come in different shapes, colors, textures, and sizes based on the type of tree from which they grow. Also, some leaves are temporary while others are more permanent and can withstand most weather conditions. How does the concept of leaves fit into our life landscape? The leaves can represent the product of the interaction between you (the trunk) and the issues and circumstances that you project unto the world (the branches). Think about a relationship or association that was more negative than positive? The end result was usually unfavorable, right? The reason this occurs is that the moment we attempt to include something in the equation that has a negative balance we have no choice but to receive a negative product. Remember learning in school that negative multiplied by a positive is always negative? The same holds true when negative energy encounters positive energy. The interesting thing is that when negative energy encounters negative energy then the product is positive.

We have all witnessed particular relationships that made us wonder what was really going on. To the outside world their interaction can be viewed as toxic but internally they are providing each other exactly what they need to feel functional within the relationship because both parties understand that they could not exist that way within a normal and healthy relationship and that they will feel out of place and overly judged. In this case, the products of this interaction cause the leaves of their branch to whither or fall off. This indicates that the branch from which the leaves are forming is somehow not conducive to positive growth.

When we start forming positive relationships, first with our inner self and then with others, we will start to see a variety of positive results. These results can be represented by leaves of either an evergreen or seasonal nature. Evergreen leaves are results that are long-lasting, such as a renewed sense of purpose, a long-term relationship, or a career move that proves to be somewhat life –changing. Seasonal leaves can also represent positive results with specific time duration such as finishing a rewarding household project, helping someone overcome a particular issue, or making a purchase that required time to plan for and to save. This scenario can also be applied to personal relationships. Sometimes we fail to recognize the fact that some attachments must be severed after the usefulness has expired. A prime example is friendship. We find that we have lifelong friends as well as those that served a purpose during a particular phase in our lives. It's safe to say that as you evolve into becoming who you are meant to become that some friends will not prove as beneficial. What you may require of friendship at eighteen may be totally different from what you may require when you approach thirty. You have to learn to be ok with those changes and understand that it doesn't speak ill of you as a person if your needs for enjoyment and fulfillment begin to change as it relates to positive growth.

Overall, leaves are the final product of your entire support system and are one of the most personal aspects of the system because it is reflective of everything that you exude either directly or as a product of yourself and another entity. The health of your leaf system is dictated by the functionality of the rest of the system. Think of it as outward projection. Every emotion, grudge, unsettled issue, and moment of joy and excitement will be portrayed through this system.

Now that you understand the significance of a sound and stable support systems as well as being honest in regards to living in your truth you are able to better recognize what is required to fulfill your emotional needs. As a result, you are able to make better choices in regards to whom and what occupies our support system. Also, expectations are now easier to form and propagate amongst your entire support system because you've taken the invaluable time required to recognize what works best for you in particular situations. At that point, members of your support system understand what is expected of them and how to react in time of need. In addition, you will more than likely become a member of someone else's support system because you have learned how to listen to yourself and recognize the positive contributions that you can offer to someone else. Your support doesn't necessarily have to be given to the people who supported you. Yet, you can honor their contributions to your life and the achievement of your goals by becoming a highly functioning vessel for someone else. Always remember that the man that believes that he acts alone is the man that is selfish to the needs of others.

CHAPTER 13
PLANNING FOR SUCCESS: PLANNING FOR LIFE

> ***Personal Pledge:*** *I will come to understand that success is not accidental. Instead, it is very much intentional and is directly related to careful planning and execution. I believe that patience serves as the fundamental ingredient to my current and future success.*

I will be the first to admit that I may be the last person that anyone would ask to write a chapter about planning for success. Then again, I feel that I can share with you my tribulations and shortcomings in terms of setting and attaining goals and how I came to resolve some of my issues associated with procrastination. I had to discover some of the causes for my procrastination in order to address the issue as a whole. What I discovered was that my procrastination was deeply rooted in my fear of failure and disappointing others.

Years ago I was told by a good friend of mine that I was a big dreamer and I remember seeing his face light up as he said it. I think he honestly felt that he was paying me a compliment. I had dreams of becoming this champion for causes very dear to my heart and to help change the world with my compassion. After he walked away I began to feel disappointment because I realized that all I had were great dreams with no clear pathway of achieving them. You can have one hundred great ideas but they are only ideas until you take the time to bring them to fruition. That means taking the time to create a roadmap for success.

I often tried to imagine myself as a result of the dreams I achieved but I could never really fathom seeing myself in that position. I later discovered that my largest barrier was my emotions. I was intelligent and resourceful enough to get what I wanted, but I did not feel that I had the emotional strength to withstand possible disappointment that usually happens when you may fail at a certain task related to a goal and I was also not patient enough to see the benefit of waiting it out when necessary. I had to find a way to make it work because I was tired of not excelling and hearing people constantly tell me that I was destined for greatness. Those around me believed in me more than I ever could at the time. The first step towards success is to feel that you are worthy and entitled to it.

Negative influences are everywhere and they can range from the subtle to the painfully obvious. I feel that my negative influences sometimes included the particular environment in which I was growing up, depending on where I lived at the time. Also, my lack of a role model in my father made it extremely hard to model myself after someone that I could look up to as well as having the necessary one-on-one access. I remember several times when my father was less encouraging of what everyone else felt were great achievements and how it either served to add fuel to my passion or extinguished what little flame was left. I was the first to finish high school, start college, and really attempt to strike out on my own. His lack of support made me feel as though I was somehow at fault for being driven and goal-oriented. Because I wanted my father in my life I began to feel as though I was deserting my family if I chose to be successful. I was allowing the sentiment of a man that had no recent positive contribution to my life control the way I viewed my potential for success. It would take years for me to understand that the problem was that he felt intimidated by anyone that achieved more than him and that his harsh words were spoken from a place that originated from his own low self-esteem. Sometimes we have to make what seem to be very emotionally difficult decisions in order to attain the success that we desire. You may find that the friends who now speak negatively of you are the ones that are not meant to share your positive journey with you. You may also find that certain family members will speak lowly about you but it's mainly because your success acts as a mirror to their insecurities and dissatisfaction with their own lives.

After I conquered the issue that esteem played on my ability to live out my dreams I had to somehow find a way to separate my dreams into something more tangible. I needed something that distinguished the seemingly hundreds of thoughts in my head into real events that stood a great chance of happening in the near or not-so-distant future. That's when I decided to use the term "goals." I've read several definitions of the word goal but the ones that resonate with me are: target, and the result of an achievement. These two terms solidified my belief that my dreams could result in achievement.

Before we begin writing our marvelous roadmaps to achieving our goals we must first ask ourselves if our goals are realistic based on our strengths and weaknesses. It may be discovered that a particular weakness must be strengthened before we begin to pursue the goal. For example, I have a goal to practice motivational speaking. The main problem is that I stutter. At the time the goal was not realistic because my stuttering problem was very prevalent and it also caused me to become very introverted and withdrawn from the public. I had to work on the issue of stuttering before I made any moves towards practicing public speaking. After putting in the necessary work to improve my vocal weakness I was then able to focus on the technicalities associated with public speaking. This was the first step in my approaching goals in a more realistic way. I knew what I was capable of at the time and I had to be honest enough to admit where the true work had to begin.

You would think that I'd be on the right track by now, right? Wrong! After putting in all of that hard work in resolving certain issues that stood in the way of my goals I now had to discover that procrastination was now my biggest enemy. Picture yourself in a marathon. You're leading the pack in what looks like an obvious win in your favor. Then, all of a sudden you find yourself losing steam midway through the race. Later, you fall behind the rest of the crew. Instead of going forward and enjoying coming in last place you decide to bow out and duck in the woods to find the quickest route back home. This was my usual action plan with any goal that seemed too far ahead of me in terms of time or the amount of work required. Anything that could be completed in a week was right up my alley but I would fall flat over any goal that took more time than I felt I could commit to it. How did I overcome this? Well, it wasn't easy and it took several dismal years of failure for me to realize what I needed in order to crack my own glass ceiling.

Most long-term goals are multi-layered. One process has to be completed before the next one can begin. I had to come to terms with the fact that some of my goals were large and long-term in nature. One of my goals was to go back to school and finish my attempt at a Bachelor's degree. But, the idea of spending several years in school part time quickly negated that goal to a mere dream. The thought still lingered in the back of my mind like a splinter located right under the skin of my thumb. I wanted the diploma but I didn't feel that I could commit the time and mental resources to making it happen. Moreover, I was afraid of starting something and not finishing it, again. I was also deathly afraid of failure as it reminded me of things I had wished for or never received in my past. I discovered that my problem was that I had to break down my goals into smaller fragments that were more workable based on my own limitations. I decided to view my educational goal as a multilayered step. I told myself I could start off by earning a certificate, which only required one year of school part-time. This was probably the best thing I had decided to do. Once I achieved the certificate I felt accomplished but unfinished. So, I decided to become a full-time college student and complete my Bachelor's degree. It was hard work as I did this while raising a very young child. But, my educational goals became deeply rooted in my desire to provide a life for my son that was not afforded to me as a child. Two months after completing my undergraduate degree I decided to enroll in graduate school. I never imagined having a graduate degree but because I took the time to discover which methods worked best for me I was able to turn my dreams into goals that were realistically attainable while putting in the work that I could manage.

This book you are reading right now is actually a very old goal of mine but I had to view the writing of this book in chapters. I would only commit to a chapter at a time and I put no pressure into creating an actual book. Sometimes I wrote feverishly for days at a time and, at other times, I found myself taking breaks that lasted for several weeks. But, I was practicing what worked for me. Not only did I create an atmosphere where I felt that I was worthy of achievement, but I was also realistic about the methods that worked best for me. It really is about working off of your best and worst attributes while gleaning from the success stories of others.

I want you to start by writing down all of your dreams and aspirations in a notebook. You can also utilize your computer and/or smart phone as well. I call this list the Dream List. Some of these dreams may seem very farfetched but the whole purpose of this exercise is to discover those aspirations that are actually attainable. After the list is finished I want you to read aloud each aspiration. My theory is that our thoughts are magnified when we write them down and either read them back to ourselves or say them aloud. We are sometimes able to rationalize certain thoughts by merely speaking them. As you are reading each aspiration I want you to take the time to evaluate it against your current capabilities and determine if the aspiration is one that is attainable. This requires honesty on your part. If you know you are limited in your abilities then now is the time to come clean. If the goal is determined to be attainable then add to a new list called GOALS. Once this is completed you are then able to view a more realistic plan for your immediate and future success. It is at this point that you can begin to chart your course of achievement.

Once you are able to identify realistic goals you now have to determine what is required to reach those goals. Remember, I stated that most goals are multi-layered and require the achievement of lower-level goals. Below is a simple worksheet that I developed and began to use with my clients in an effort to integrate visual stimulation so that they are able to document their goals and plan their progress. It is called the GOAL ACTUALIZATION WORKSHEET (next page).

GOAL ACTUALIZATION WORKSHEET

GOAL	STEP 1	STEP 2	STEP 3
Buy a new car	Save money for down payment	Make sure trade-in is in good shape	Obtain at least three reasonable offers before making a decision
Start College	Decide my subject of interest	Submit application by deadline	Make decision as to which school to attend
Lose 15 lbs.	Research weight management plans	Make necessary dietary changes	Create a manageable exercise regimen

Simply put, this worksheet provides a visual overview of the goals that were determined to be realistic based on the dream list that you previously put together. The column to the far left is used to document each goal using abstract terms. I use terms such as "buy a new car" or "start college" to state the overall goal. The details are built into the steps required to achieve the goal. Next, each goal has at least one step. I've taken the liberty of listing only three steps per goal for presentation purposes but some goals may require only one step while some may require more than three. It is dictated strictly by the goal and what is required. You may find that certain steps can be omitted while some steps are absolute necessary. This list does not have to be static, in that it can change as necessary. The goal is to create the regimen of documenting your goals so that they all exist in one place. By creating a checklist such as this you are learning to hold yourself accountable and putting the responsibility upon yourself.

We are continuing our practice of journaling which also allows you to develop the trust that one should have with their own spirit and intuition. This trust acts as a protective mechanism and allows us to prioritize our needs and remove the chaos that usually comes with an abundant amount of thinking. The thoughts are still there but there is safety in knowing that the ideas are continuously documented and therefore retrievable. At that point you can free your mind to explore other thoughts and ideas as necessary.

Another method that helped me to either achieve or plan for my goals was to surround myself with people that were engaging in something similar to what I had hoped to achieve. I would befriend authors that were committed to their passion and I fed off of their patience, determination, and energy. These same people were usually upbeat about life in general and made their support for my dreams very prominent. I often felt that they had a greater belief in me than I did. Overall, I felt that I was being emotionally mentored by these groups of people. I didn't feel intimidated and they were very open in sharing their path to success. This was a far cry from some of the people I had the displeasure of encountering. There were times where my questions were met with cold looks and I felt that some people were threatened by my curiosity in regards to their success. Maybe they were afraid that I would surpass them. I had no desire to surpass anyone. My only desire was to surpass my own expectations, and as such, I had to find a way to surround myself with people that held the same views of success.

Now that we have a great list of goals to work from we must now concentrate our efforts on creating a roadmap for each goal. One roadmap may include reaching one of the goals on your list that coincidentally prepares you for the next goal. For example, one of my goals was to eventually enter the management arena within the information technology industry. I felt that obtaining my Master's degree in management would put me on the right track for that to happen. So, by reaching the goal of obtaining my Master's degree I automatically prepared myself to reach the next goal. I tend to use education as one of my main examples these days and I think it's because expanding one's knowledgebase, in any form, is one of the most realistic goals that most people feel is bond their reach. Education can be obtained from so many sources nowadays that we find ourselves learning when we don't realize we are and I feel that everyone has some capacity to learn, especially once we discover our own comfort zone that is conducive to learning. Also, by expanding our mental boundaries it offers us a subconscious level of confidence that gives us more freedom to expound on other goals that we've yet to put forth an effort.

For everything we wish to achieve we should also prepare ourselves to put forth the effort in terms of research. For example, if your goal is to become a party planner then you should invest your time in researching the steps required to advance to that designation. Those steps can include researching training options or joining particular organizations or associations that cater to your specific interest. What matters is that you align yourself with the right resources that increase the likelihood of you attaining your goal. Your resources can include people, locations, and education. I have had the inspiration to write this book for years but I knew that I was not ready to take on the challenge because I had not aligned myself with the correct resources to begin this journey. I knew of no other authors from whom I could glean any helpful advice. I felt that authoring was in my nature but I wasn't even sure of what story I would be compelled to tell. So, I had to make an earnest attempt to perform research on the topic of authoring. Writing is easy but authoring a novel is an entirely different beast within itself. I invested several years of watching the pros and learning myself well enough to discover the story that I felt I needed to tell. I had no idea that my first book would actually come from my own experiences.

You may find yourself trying a few different ways to get to one single goal and that is perfectly ok. You will also find that everything may seem difficult at first, including the thought process and mapping out your plan of action. That's only because it is new to you and not in your usual set of actions.

Prepare yourself for those times that you face adversity. There may be disappointments at varying levels throughout your quest for achievement but rest assured that a good disaster recovery plan helps to alleviate the fallout that occurs after unexpected setbacks that may occur.

Working in the field of information technology makes me no stranger to disaster recovery planning. In short, disaster recovery refers to the action or set of actions that are put in place when disaster happens so that the overall effect is less damaging. It is important to have a plan of action just in case the actions you take to achieve your goal suddenly go awry. This will allow you to bounce back in a much more effective manner without taking you further off course than necessary. I fondly remember applying to graduate school and the nerve-wracking process of completing essays and personal questions. I had my eye on this one particular school; it was an ivy-league school and the curriculum that I wanted to study was known worldwide. While awaiting the decision regarding my acceptance I decided that if I did not get accepted that I was going to continue my graduate studies at the same school where I received my undergraduate degree. Well, as luck would have it, I did not get accepted into the graduate program of my choice. I was disappointed for a moment but I realized that I had a disaster recovery plan. I had begun my graduate studies at my undergraduate alma mater in what seemed like no time at all and without further disappointment.

The best part about trying different methods is that you will come to know what works best based on your personality and strengths. You will come to find that you struggle less with methods that are of no benefit and you will waste less time procrastinating because the trial and error will assist in eliminating fear and apprehension. Also, you will fully understand your present boundaries and find out whether those boundaries are fine the way that they are or if it is possible to expand those boundaries so long as it is within your personal comfort level. I usually tell people that what may be good for you may not be good for me. We can come to the same destination while taking a different route to get there. Just know that if your way of carrying out the steps necessary to reach your goals sits well with your spirit then that's all that really matters. I sometimes take the long road because I enjoy discovering alternate paths to the same destination. Maybe I just enjoy taking the scenic route. The beautiful details of the trees are sometimes as captivating as the view of the entire forest. So, take time to enjoy the journey to betterment instead of only focusing on the end result.

The primary learning objective is that taking the first step is usually the hardest. But, once that first step is taken it becomes less difficult to take that second, third, and fourth step. Pretty soon you will find yourself running and anxious to reach that finish line. Remember, you learn to crawl before you learn to walk, so allow yourself the necessary time to become a master at creating your own personally defined roadmaps for success. It has to work for you in order to be of a benefit to you. Every goal begins with a thought that is supported by desire, passion, and hard work.

Below is a 10-step guide that I've formulated that may assist you with staying focused and energized to proceed with any goal that you are contemplating:

1. **Make the decision to take the first step:**

The simple thought of taking on a new goal may evoke instant fear. It is the fear of change and/or of the unknown that strikes deep for some. Remember that God created you in His image and that you are as deserving of prosperity as the person who has already achieved what you want to achieve. No human can undermine God's plan for you. Even with the most well thought out plan some of us will be afraid of that first step because it translates to a new commitment and a step in a direction that one's esteem may find difficult to accept. When you commit to taking the first step it is likely that you will find it easier to commit to the succeeding steps. Remember that you are never alone as you drive towards your goal. God has a permanent seat on the passenger side and is only waiting to be acknowledged as the most important member of your support team.

2. All goals require a plan and a pace that fits your current lifestyle:

Every great result usually requires a great plan of action. In fact, a plan of action sometimes takes longer to develop than the actual tasks that will be performed, but it is always important to have some type of plan that will serve as your checklist or some form of accountability for your activities. Also, discover a pace that fits your current way of life so that it does not create an additional roadblock or esteem blocker.

3. Understand which goals can be attempted simultaneously and those that must be completed individually

Almost everyone is familiar with the daunting task of managing multiple tasks or goals at one time. Unfortunately, not knowing which tasks can be managed simultaneously can result in unnecessary stress and can make one feel helpless. It is important to decide which goals can be either attempted simultaneously or require isolation and the most of your attention considering every other task or responsibility that you have to complete. Achievement on any level is cause to celebrate. It is true that we have the ability to multitask, but there is a difference between multitasking and overburdening ourselves to a point where the stress of it all can cause us both mental and physical anguish

4. Self-Motivation and Positive Self-Talk is paramount to your success:

Come up with clever ways to keep yourself motivated to stay on the right path to success. For example, write positive words of affirmation on sticky notes and attach them to places that you are likely to visit daily such as a bedroom or bathroom mirror, refrigerator, or at the edge of your monitor at your work desk. You can also create a screen saver on your computer or cellular phone that reminds you to stay on track and that you are fully capable of reaching any goal. Positive self-talk includes any verbal confirmation that you give to yourself at the pivotal moments that may make the difference between pushing forward and giving up. Remind yourself that you were born a winner and that you have all of the resources available to reach your mark. You may not believe it initially but you will begin to reprogram your frame of thought and eventually it will aid you in the home stretch.

5. Understand that PATIENCE truly is a virtue during this time:

Research states that a habit takes at last three weeks to form. So, do not be dismayed if you find it extremely difficult in the beginning to successfully enact the changes required to meet a certain goal. This is a test of your will power but should not be viewed as a deterrent to your success. You are more than likely attempting to reprogram many years of life training which is rarely ever an easy feat. Create a plan to evoke small and gradual changes that will become less formal and more habit over time. Also, expect moments that may cause you to backslide but do not accept defeat. Try again and again until you discover a method that works for your personality.

6. Emulate those that are doing or have done what you are attempting to achieve:

Sometimes the best roadmap to success is those that have come before you and who are doing what you do very well. Seek role models who exemplify the behavior that you are hoping to emulate. Also, investigate their life story. You may find additional similarities between your own struggles and the struggles that they also felt were insurmountable. You will come to realize that every adversity makes room for valuable lessons to be learned and can build character and strength if the decision is made to overcome the situation.

7. *Form a reliable and sustainable support system:*

A healthy support system is one of the most important components that can greatly improve your ability to stay on course with achieving your goals. A highly functioning support system should provide the following benefits: support to your esteem, help create accountability, and provide honest and compassionate feedback. You will undoubtedly have days where your determination will sway from high to low so it is always great to have a network of people to rely upon in those times of emotional need. The simplest of changes you decide to apply to your lifestyle can be difficult to cope with so don't attempt to do it alone if you absolutely do not have to. Consider people you know that have your best interest at heart and to whom you are willing to be accountable. Also, make yourself available to constructive feedback and be wary of discouraging actions from others who may not be personally invested in your success.

8. *Substitute positive replacements for negative behaviors:*

Usually the game plan that you have devised to achieve a specific goal may also include the elimination of negative behaviors that prove counteractive to the new goals that we have set. I want you to think about some of your most counterproductive habits. Next, consider more positive behaviors that can serve as a replacement. Then, incorporate the substitutions one by one until each alternative action becomes a permanent solution. If you find out extremely difficult to replace counterproductive behaviors with more beneficial behaviors

9. Celebrate and be proud of yourself at each level of achievement.

This is directly linked to having patience when pursuing your goals as well as learning to celebrate yourself as you proceed with the positive changes that you have promised to yourself. Often times we lose motivation when we do not see results as quickly as we should. It's the "all or nothing" mentality that makes us feel that the only moments worthy of celebration are the moments of completion. Set milestones or smaller areas of achievement within a major goal that allows moments for celebration. This will help to strengthen your reliance on self-motivation as opposed to exterior motivation. This celebration process helps to renew the energy required to move on to the next milestone and will immediately affect your personal disposition. Others will eventually notice as well.

10. *Prepare yourself to embrace your new changes:*

Believe it or not, many people want to make positive changes, but are not equipped to embrace the changes that are outside of their purview or immediate vision which is usually influenced by current or lingering circumstances. Once we decide to enact positive change we must also prepare ourselves to accept the changes that will occur. People may treat you differently because of your success. Either they will be deterred by your self-confidence or they will welcome it with open arms. Also, you will more than likely attract different types of people along with different opportunities. That's the entire point of change; to allow yourself the opportunity to walk faithfully into your future and accept the blessings that come with positive change.

Now, I want to see you approach your newly-defined goals with a plan that is reasonable based on your available of time and resources, a great support system, renewed vigor, and the outlook that allows you to see the victory line before you've attempted the first task. See you at the finish line!

"The road less traveled represents obstacles you have yet to encounter. Potholes, fallen trees, and debris represent past hurts, haunts, and unexpected turmoil that are meant to deter you from your original path to personal success. Ultimately, a different path to the same destination is waiting to be discovered. It is that different and unfamiliar path that will lead you to renewal of strength, confidence, and innovation. Be prepared to become uncomfortable for the sake of personal gain."

CHAPTER 14

DRIVING BEYOND THE STOP SIGNS

> ***Personal Pledge:*** *I understand that life consists of many roads less traveled. I will attempt to establish alternate paths to success and will no longer allow myself to be permanently diverted as long as other options exist.*

Sometimes, the biggest deterrent in our efforts to move forward is our inability to move past the curve balls that life can and will toss our way. Everyone handles these occurrences differently. Some of us instantly switch gears with the end goal remaining intact while others begin to sink slowly in quick sand because they feel imprisoned in indecision. I'd like you to take a moment and think back to your last major road trip, either as a driver or passenger. You more than likely attempted to assure the success of your trip by equipping yourself and your vehicle with more than the essentials such as a well-inflated spare tire, first aid kit, some food for travel, a flashlight, and enough cash and credit on hand just in case of an unexpected emergency. With possible detours and sharp curves abound you confidently brave the course that leads to your final destination. You will more than likely also encounter several stop signs and signal lights along the way but you react to them as you usually do, with confident precision. The interesting thing is that most of us find it difficult to maneuver the detours and blockades in our lives. In most cases it boils down to your perspective of your situations.

You know the old question "is the glass half empty or half full"? The optimists would answer that it is half full and believe that achievement can be found in the fragments that comprise the total goal. The pessimist would argue that it is half empty and focus on the supposed loss or incompletion that still exists. Again, it's all about perspective.

Earlier, I wrote about accepting your reality and deciding whether that reality was healthy enough to remain as it was or if it proves disastrous to your outlook on life, therefore requiring a change. Six years ago I would have quickly answered that the glass was half empty due to the fact that I felt incomplete and anything that represented something either unfinished or incomplete was a subconscious reminder of the many remnants of my life that never came together to form one vision or clear outlook. While in that position I felt that my view was outside of my control. It was as if I knew that my will was not strong enough to persuade my mind to alter its view of any circumstance I faced. Then, it became a habitual part of my lifestyle and later it became something that consumed my life.

Great dreams of my own were cut off at the neck even when fair attempts were made to turn them into reality. I also deprived myself of the valuable lessons to be found in defeat or otherwise disappointing moments. How do YOU handle the sharp curves, unexpected detours, and road closures that will happen during your lifetime? Will your life come to a standstill while you regroup in order to attempt to continue down the road or will you feel confident enough to continue in your usual fashion? The answer should be the latter. You want to be able to traverse life's obstacles as if your reactions are second nature especially if those obstacles are usually easy to overcome.

My losses, either simple or great, were usually met with almost a complete stoppage. In my mind I would ask myself "what do I do now?" I remember being unable to think of anything else but the situation at hand and as a result becoming stuck in the initial shock related to change. I was afraid of anything that challenged the comfort zone that I attempted to create for myself. I knew that my comfort zone was not always the best for me but the zone and everything contained in it were reliable. I knew how to react to usual circumstances and I trained myself to believe that I was ok with the way things were. Growth wasn't an option and I rebelled against anything that challenged "the zone". This phenomenon is common amongst individuals that have attempted to deal with the type of adversities that result in the conditioning of what is safe and unsafe. This is why detours are very unnerving because it challenges us and in our minds we are made to feel that our way of thinking is wrong and that it is an additional tool used to judge us in a negative way. As a result, we immediately react with resistance to any new idea no matter if the idea is meant to move us in the right direction and into an area of positive breakthrough.

Dealing with the issues associated with my relationship with my biological father usually ended up testing my patience and my capacity to sincerely hate someone. After each attempt to remedy the different situations that put a strain on our relationship I usually felt emotionally beaten and drained. Each incident left me more confused and dismayed than the previous one because I attempt to use emotional pleas to get my points across. As usual, I was made to feel that my feelings were irrational although everyone else knew the truth. I never stopped to realize that I was traveling down the same road and expecting some type of alternate destination. If the players in the game are all the same and neither one of us has grown to understand the other person then how could I have expected anything different? At some point I realized that I needed to somehow purge these feelings from my spirit but I knew that I could no longer make similar attempts as I had in the past. One of the hardest things for me to do was to try something different. I felt sure in knowing that I was not wrong about my feelings and that he should accept them and react the way that I needed to react.

As I mentioned previously, I had to understand that he is the man that he is and it truly has nothing to do with me because I was not the only one who had similar experiences. The difference between me and others was that they accepted who he was and I felt the need to change him. I decided to try an alternate route and give in to the fact that things will not change between us and that I will continue to hurt myself by expecting more than I should from this person. So, as hard as it was, I decided to accept him the way that he was. Also, I decided that he did not deserve to impact my life in the manner that I had allowed him to up to that point. After making these decisions I realized that I had so much power over the situation from the start but I was the only one who could have brought myself to this realization. My decision to try an alternate route proved to be the best thing in this situation. I was able to exert control in an area whereby I repeatedly relinquished it in hopes of expecting a different result.

One of the reasons why we sometimes allow our lives to come to a complete halt when faced with unexpected results is because we sit in repeated judgment of the actions that have led us to the stop sign. Another reason is related to our inability to see that deterrence doesn't always translate into a complete stop. A disruption in one's usual way of thinking and moving can cause catastrophic results because usually there isn't an alternate train of thought prepared to deal with the disruption. Unfortunately, disruptions happen to everyone. Some sail right through and able to redirect their energy in a different direction but not without suffering a few scratches and perhaps a flat tire or two. Others become paralyzed and instantly think in terms of failure or missed opportunity.

Every habit or process that one enacts in a cyclic manner becomes more of a personal definition. For example, your routine at work is better when it is left undisturbed and your weekly appointment with your trainer goes well when he or she is on time. Or, you have a much better time on dates when you are totally clear on what is expected to happen. Every now and again something comes along to shake up the routine or pattern of expectations. That shake-up may serve as the spark for growth that would not have otherwise occurred.

When a detour occurs along a driving path you are usually given instructions for alternate routes. Then, the choice is yours as to whether or not you return to your point of origin or to choose amongst the choices you were given. We almost always choose an alternate route because we still must get to that destination. Of course, the alternate route may lead to a delay of some sort. If the delay is great then we would probably somehow send a message to someone if they are awaiting our arrival at a particular time. The fact is that we eventually reach our destination; all parties involved have been made aware of the situation and life proceeds as normal. If only we could apply these principles to the roadblocks that occur in our lives.

Some of us tend to think that every road block in life is a personal attack towards our own personal opinion or mode of operation. Imagine a situation at work where there was a change in policy that affected your usual way of doing business. This disruption may be fine for others to handle but you may choose a more negative mechanism of coping. Then, as usual, you begin the questioning of whether or not it was a personal attack, and if so, by whom? By doing this you have already set the stage for more negative reactions. Sooner or later, the situation becomes much larger than originally intended and you are left with the majority of the bill for its escalation. The majority of the other employees may have taken issue with the policy merely because it was a change in the way that business was usually done but it did not come at a cost of any drastic change that would infringe on anyone's ability to perform the work. In essence, it should have involved on a small amount of change management and not the negative reaction that was exhibited. Too much time was wasted on the REACTION as opposed to being fully invested and committed to the SOLUTION.

Change is inevitable and it is exhibited in almost every day that we are fortunate enough to experience. But, change should not always be perceived as always negatively disruptive. Sometimes change can be used to stretch our perception of a very limited view of reality. Those of us with highly defensive personalities will almost always perceive change as an intentional nudge at our beliefs and routines instead of viewing it as an opportunity to grow. For example, you may complain that you have been passed over for a promotion and take offense to the fact that someone with less tenure received the promotion. Maybe that individual was positively responsive to change which may have been a requirement of the new position. When change or a disruption of a usual routine presented itself that individual may have taken the initiative to immediately recognize either a remedy to the situation or finding ways to make the change work in their favor. The most important lesson to learn from this example is that it is important to learn why you are reacting the way you do as opposed to reacting just because it's what you've always done.

Just like the example given of the road detour, we almost always have alternate paths either towards the completion of a goal or our response to change. In fact, having or being forced to consider an alternate path empowers us with an enhanced level of understanding of just how our goals are intricately related to another. Each achievement makes it that much easier to pursue the next one with more vigor and determination because careful planning will have been done to help insure a higher level of success. Our level of resilience is magnified and we are less deterred by things that seem either trivial or non-threatening. If we take the time to evaluate each obstacle as its own entity we will more than likely understand the importance of its occurrence such as whether it leads to a bigger discovery about ourselves that we would have otherwise ignored.

I'd like to mention that it is also important to trust the opinions of others that you trust. To this day I find joy in knowing that if I was to take my problem to someone that I trust that I am almost sure to come away either with confirmation that I am pursuing the right path or discovering an alternative way of thinking about the situation. Sometimes, the alternative may not be as much an opposite idea as we assumed it would be but it does open up the possibility that maybe we are pursuing solutions that are in the right direction.

We have to be open-minded enough to inquire about alternate modes of thinking. We usually forget that valuable forms of assistance exist within our family, circle of friends and associates. Also, by enlisting the help of others we begin to show appreciation to those that hope to have a valuable contribution to our lives. You are creating more value than you previously knew existed as well as building an alliance between yourself and those that make up your support system while creating a mechanism of coping that begins to rank situations at different levels and deal with them according to their level of priority and impact on your life.

Whenever roadblocks occur you learn to first depend on yourself for the answer then decide what part of your support system to rely on for those areas that are unfamiliar. It is also preferable to receive and accept more than one alternate course of action. You want to feel that the alternate course is in line with who you are as a person so that there are fewer moments of inconsistency and confusion. At some point the inconsistency and confusion presented by taking an alternate route will become more familiar and less fearful. In the end you will have added a new solution to the same problem.

This type of thinking is not engrained overnight and will take as long as you allow it to take. I sometimes still find myself in situations that leave me breathless and seemingly without recourse but I have to try my best to remember that the worst thing I could do is to NOT allow myself to think outside of my own box in order to help myself first. It's time you allowed yourself the opportunity to view your options in a more vivid light than you ever felt existed before. This world was built upon millions of problems that were accompanied by millions of solutions so do not discount your ability to think of a few alternate solutions here and there when necessary. Consider it an investment in a life well-traveled.

Sometimes, that stop sign that has been placed ahead of you serves as God's attempt to separate you from what you've always done in hopes of graduating you to a routine that results in something brand new and sometimes unexpected. Most of us travel down the same path because it is familiar while ignoring the fact that what was familiar may have never worked in your favor. Sure, there is comfort in what is familiar but we have all been in positions whereby comfort does not necessarily translate into growth or anything positive. We become comfortable, and sometimes lazy, because we know what is to be expected and are terrified of taking an obvious detour that will result in a different perspective. That stop sign ahead may represent the change that you have prayed and supposedly worked hard for yet the fear of the unknown has stopped you dead in your tracks and paralyzed your ability to see further than NOW.

That stop sign may represent the moment that requires a crucial decision to be made is at relates to your personal welfare. For example, it can represent the decision to finally take the steps necessary to leave an abusive relationship that you continuously return to with the thought of it getting better. The truth is that you did not return to that relationship because you hope it would get better. You already know that it won't get any better as long as you return to something that is the same as you left it. You returned because it is what you know and what you have grown accustomed to. This is not to say that you want to be abused. However, it is to say that you TRUST THE CONSISTENCY of whatever that relationship has become. That stop sign can also represent the decision to stop being the abuser in the relationship. The regret that exists in your spirit after the altercation is an indicator that you no longer want to be in the position to purposely hurt another individual yet your responses to adversity are always the same. You apologize repeatedly while making promises to change and relinquish the behavior without realizing that the person on the other end of the assault actually doesn't believe a word that is coming out of your mouth. When you are truly tired of feeling regret over your actions and exhausted from inflicting pain upon others that you confuse as control you will walk down that different path or open that "other" door to new actions and expectations that will result in a new way of operating within your life.

That stop sign coming up at the intersection ahead can serve as a reminder that you have choices to make as it relates to your ultimate destination or your well-being. That choice can be as simple as either life or death. The drug habit that has had you bound for years is only a symptom of a much larger vulnerability that existed before you took that first hit. What started as a means of altering your mood so that you may get through your seemingly unbearable day has turned into a full-blown physical war with yourself that has you teetering on the brink of total destruction. You've lost your home, job, car, children, and other heartfelt assets that should otherwise bring you joy and have been robbed of the will that most of us take for granted every day. You can't simply say "NO" to getting high again. In order for you to begin the journey to a sober life you have to make the decision to twist that doorknob and open the door to resources that are in place to help you rediscover the person that God intended you to be; a fully viable human being made in his image that is capable of conquering any adversity placed in front of you if the right choices are made. I understand that you blame yourself or other circumstances for your predicament. I also understand that you deny the fact that you can't control what you refuse to call a problem. But, blame and denial is getting you absolutely nowhere at this point. Each hit represents your walk down the same road with the exception that your feet have become more bruised with each pass. Your body is growing tired and weak from the repetitive walk down that same street. The only choices at your disposal are survival or death and each choice requires a different path. Either choice comes with the risk of failure that one must accept but the possible gains earned on the side of survival far outweigh the immediate gains that an immediate and temporary fix can offer.

That stop sign that stands between your choices to either continue the pursuit your life-long dream or to throw in the towel may have been placed there to test your strength, patience, and determination. You may come to find that the dream was short lived or that you must do whatever it takes to satisfy your lifelong desires despite occasional obstructions. Often times we create lofty dreams and goals without understanding how much of an undertaking is required to bring those same dreams and goals to fruition. For some of us it may take years to capture the crown and to understand the purpose of our investment of hard work, time, patience, and finances. Other people may doubt your ability to succeed but their doubt in you can serve as continued fuel for motivation. Besides, no one can resist the moment that you can proudly say "look at me now". Don't sell yourself short. God has made provisions for you to live a fully realized and satisfied life and sometimes we have to take extra steps beyond our comfort zone to reach that next level of achievement and personal healing.

CHAPTER 15
WALKING A MILE IN AUNT BRENDA'S SHOES

There comes a point in time when those that judge for the sake of tearing others down become the judged and are left to sit alone and await the rendering of opinions, which in most cases never really matter to begin with. Sometimes it takes one to fall down their well of despair and confusion in order to understand that at times the reasons behind the decisions we make may far outweigh the actions that resulted in certain consequences. I asked God for further enlightenment that would enhance my ability to be of great help to others in times of need. As a result, I was sent through a journey that although brief, opened my eyes to a deeper level of sincerity and compassion.

As my introduction to an otherwise bright and sunny morning on Sunday, December 2, 2012, I found myself lying in the fetal position in bed with an irresolvable pain radiating from my mouth to my head, fading in and out of reality, while feeling completely helpless. I had been suffering from what I thought was a simple toothache for about two weeks and the pain had become so severe that I was literally hoping I would black out so that the torture could be forgotten. The initial comfort of over-the-counter medications had begun to dissipate as the pain grew more and more resistant by the minute. I stubbornly refused to visit a dentist. I don't recall anyone, especially members of my immediate family, enjoyed visiting the dentist. I think it's because we feel that it is the mission of all dentists to find something wrong, even if nothing is. Personally, I feel that they get a cheap thrill every time they are able to drill into or extract something. I've often thought I heard them chuckle under their masks as a sign of hidden pleasure at my displayed discomfort. What began as a six month noninvasive cleaning procedure would usually turn into a laundry list of procedures that, if told only from a dentist point of view, would render you toothless if you refused to submit to the numerous procedures. Needless to say, this mentality fostered my desire to NOT to see the dentist. Adding confusion to my situation was the fact that the pain felt as though it was coming from below a crown that was put in place several years ago. It was now time to reach out for help regardless of the source of the pain.

Although I knew I was in excruciating pain I felt there was something more sinister at play inside of me, something I just could not pinpoint. Barely able to think straight I was literally forgetting where I was at times. I rang the phone of my ex and asked for assistance in getting to the nearest hospital. I remember being unable to walk to the vehicle without assistance and also having to recline the seat all the way to the floor in order to feel some type of comfort. I do not remember much of the drive to the hospital as I was forcing myself to think happy thoughts of my children and other pleasurable memories in order to help me deal with the pain and other symptoms I was facing. Upon arriving to the emergency room of the hospital I informed the front desk person about my hypertension and that the pain could possibly be affecting my blood pressure. I knew from prior experience that the mention of a possible spike in blood pressure would move you closer to the front of the line for check-in as well as to be seen by an emergency room physician.

I was rushed through the check-in process, where my vital signs were recorded. I remember the nurse stating that my blood pressure was extremely high as I was explaining to her what prompted my visit to the emergency room that day. I was then escorted to the waiting area for what seemed to be no more than a few minutes before I heard my name being called again to come to the emergency area. I was placed on a bed and was asked to repeat what had prompted my visit. Now, this is the moment where I had to pray for complete sanity because in my head I am swearing more than I remember ever swearing at one time because I did not want to open my mouth for any reason. The slightest hint of cool air felt like a crowbar being leveled on my head and mouth. I knew I had just explained to the registration nurse what happened and now I had to find the strength to pry my jaws open, exposing my teeth and gums to the frigid cold of the hospital cooling system, and again explain the reason that brought me here. All thoughts of candor quickly began to escape my mind, but somehow I had to hold it together and attempt to relay as much information as I could muster in order to receive the help I so desperately desired. While giving my statement I happened to glance over my shoulder and what I saw shook me to the core. My blood pressure reading at that moment was 220/130. In other words, I could, at any moment, experience either a heart attack or stroke more than likely resulting in either the last day my soul resided within this body or severe impairment.

In the midst of a crisis your life sometimes flashes before you in an instant. My first thoughts were those of my sons and the memories that were yet to be created. I so enjoyed being their dad that I could not fathom not fulfilling this role as long as possible. I instantly recalled the moment that the social worker arrived with Tyler, who was two weeks old at the time. I also recalled pulling back the blanket that covered his face while he sat in the infant carrier. Our eyes met and I knew I would love him completely from that moment on. I began to recall birthday parties and special milestones that I'm almost sure every parent can relate to. I felt myself instantly missing my kids, as if I had already checked out. While looking at the doctor's face I remember reciting a prayer to myself asking God to spare my life because my work here was not done yet. Uncontrollably, I yelled "please give me something for the pain". I heard the doctor mention morphine to the nurse. I remember hearing about morphine and its usage in cases of extreme pain. At that point they could've told me they were giving me mud in a cup, I didn't care, as long as it would help to relieve me of this excruciating pain. Then my head began to throb violently and my already-shaky vision becoming even shakier. I then begged for morphine. The doctor agreed and motioned for the nurse to administer a dosage. . She injected the medication into my IV bottle and within a couple of seconds I could feel a warm sensation run through my chest. It wasn't painful nor uncomfortable; just different. Within a few seconds I was pain free. It was as if the gates of heaven had opened up and God had put his index finger on my forehead and said "there you go my child". Previous days of pain were virtually wiped off of my record with one injection. All I could think about was how I could get more because I knew that the high would eventually fade.

It was decided that I would be admitted into the hospital, at least for overnight observation due to my high blood pressure. I willingly submitted without objection, just as long as I received my next hit of morphine or any other available high-dosage pain relief. A few hours later I could feel the effects of the morphine dissipate so I rang the button to summon a nurse. Once she arrived I requested more morphine but to my surprise I was informed I had reached limit of this wonderful drug. You could've knocked me over with a feather for I was certain that I would be doped up all night until my release. For a short moment I became bitter and reluctant to hear anything else she had to say. I wanted relief and I wanted what I knew worked. Then she offered me an alternative that served as my introduction to the wondrous, and highly addictive, world of Percocet. I had heard about the drug before and had known it to be highly habit forming but for the sake of that night, I was willing to try anything for relief and a good night's sleep.

Besides pain relief I also felt that my natural personality was being heavily subdued. It was as if I had become someone new, someone I had never met before and I wasn't sure how to feel about that. I couldn't come up with a quick one-liner to make the nurses laugh nor could I muster one inspirational saying, not even if it was targeted at me. On one hand I felt relaxed and pain-free, but on the other hand I felt my usually-comical and jovial spirit slowly slip away. The relief from the pain was continuing to help bring down my dangerously high blood pressure so at that moment in time, it was a win-win situation on both sides of the coin. I could still feel "me" slowly slipping away. The reality I once knew was becoming skewed by physical satisfaction that proved to be only temporary. Over the course of the night and late morning I received another dosage of Percocet before being processed for released from the hospital.

Before I was to leave my hospital room I had warned the nurse that I was not feeling well. This had nothing to do with any pain I was feeling, but more in regards to not feeling like myself. I was told that I may be a little groggy and that it should wear off shortly. With the assistance of a nurse I walked out of my room and began to walk down the hall. I knew something was not right and I told the nurse again that I did not feel well at all. I took another twenty steps or so outside of the room. Then, I remembered feeling extremely lightheaded and a cold sweat had overcome my body in a matter of seconds. I could no longer stand. I immediately fell to the floor. Nurses and doctors scurried from behind their stations to assist, picking me up and bringing me back to my room and getting me back in bed. I remember thinking to myself "am I having withdrawals from the drugs I had been given?" It was at that moment that I remembered living through my Aunt Brenda's drug addiction; watching her mentally and physically deteriorate as the disease took over and rendering her helpless in her own fight.

I came to realize that I was not having withdrawal symptoms but the fact that I was not capable of caring for myself suddenly made the throws of her addiction that much easier for me to understand. In less than twenty four hours I had been subject to an experience that created a vulnerability so strong that had me willing to do and try anything that would offer relief and pacification. Once the relief had been given I was afraid to face life without it. I needed the next fix to make me feel "normal". Then, after some point I was wanting it as much as I could possibly get it. I would have made agreements with shady characters or performed shady deals just to get my hands on anything that would relieve the pain. Then when it was taken away I was subject to the original pain all over again.

I had already come to the conclusion that the start of her drug addiction had little to do with the addiction itself and everything to do with some form of vulnerability that made it easier for her to make the decision to use crack. I now feel that it was God's way of helping me understand that at some point I was judging the wrong parts of HER equation and that no parts of her addiction affected the love she had for me. But I took it personally because I loved her so much. I had absolutely no doubt that she loved me just as much. Sure, I had forgiven her years ago and felt that I was more open-minded, having lived through that ordeal but I had now become more open-minded having lived through an example of the ordeal. I was given an unsolicited opportunity to walk a mile in her shoes, though my version of this walk fell short a few hundred miles in comparison. I began to recount the journey of her life as a whole and came to a deeper understanding of the moving parts that created an opening for her to feel as though she needed that first hit. Recalling the tales of her life including becoming a teenage mother at age fifteen and again at sixteen, suffering through at least one physically abusive relationship, losing her mother (her rock) unexpectedly, and other situations that I am sure I was not privy to led me to understand that behind the smiles, affection, and gratitude that she gave everyone was a troubled soul that just wanted in return what she gave to us. Unfortunately, we weren't always successful in understanding what she needed and that was unconditional love and a true understanding of her situation.

The ordeal that I experienced made me more determined to help myself because I had come face to face with a vulnerability that was so overpowering that I could've easily made the same choices so others have made; to extinguish pain with remedies that would eventually end up doing much more extreme harm than good. I could not see myself in her position or being forced to make decisions as such. So, after my release from the hospital I immediately scheduled a dentist appointment, received antibiotics for the infection, then had the tooth removed which resolved the problem. The take away from the entire ordeal is that judgment of others, without knowing the full story of what led to their actions, can be dangerously negative and serves the least benefit to those that I am trying to help. It also brings to light the importance of asking the right questions so that one can feel safe enough to open up in ways that felt that they may have never been allowed to before.

We've all had judgments leveled against us for the choices we made even when the choices were some that we probably would not have made had the circumstances presented themselves differently. We pass judgment against others for their choices of life mate, career, or activities that for them seem recreational and fun but to us can be viewed as reckless and nonproductive. The choices that we make are a direct result of how we feel about ourselves in terms of what we deserve and how far in the future we are able to see ourselves. But, are we asking the right questions? It can be as simple as asking what does one feel when engaging in a certain activity.

The respect of one's life story is also crucial in the process of bringing someone towards the brightest and most productive parts of their spirit. When you listen and respect someone's story they are more willing to divulge truths that lay dormant out of fear of persecution or rejection, even if some of the situation were clearly out of their control. It can make the difference between forcing one's inner child back into a dark corner to only rear its presence through either self-destructive or nonproductive actions or allowing that inner child to mature into a positively functioning, highly self-aware, and confident adult that will understand that mistakes are a part of our entire life cycle but what matters most is our ability to accept what has happened and move forward with a new understanding of how to prevent them from happening again.

If we truly want to be of help to one another we have to be able to set aside our personal feelings of what we feel others should be doing with their lives and realize that in most cases it has absolutely nothing to do with us personally but everything to do with an internalization of deservedness and personal strength. When we are able to not only understand but also fully accept the full story that has influenced one's convictions and actions, we can then put ourselves in their shoes and perhaps say "I get why you would have made that choice but now let me help you understand why you deserve everything that God has in store for you". Truly, what God has in store for is always better than we can ever imagine. But we cannot reach the bounty of what has been provisioned for us unless we are prepared to make better choices that lead us down the right path. To judge is a human condition that we can't escape but the severity of how we judge is the culprit of most of our failures as it relates to acting as a true means of support for our fellow man.

I can remember the years that our family was plagued with my aunt's drug addiction. Ironically, that side of the family also had its share of alcoholics, chain smokers, and a few pedophiles that went unpunished but for some reason her addiction was more profound than any of the other issues I just mentioned. I feel it has to do with the fact that drinking and smoking is more acceptable and the pedophilia was covered up because some felt it would bring shame to the family. I can remember relatives lashing out at her negatively just to spite her by hurling out very hateful insults. Never once did they consider that those insults were not making it any easier for her to make better choices. In fact, I would not be surprised if it caused her to sink lower in her addiction. At least the drugs didn't judge her. We took her addiction personally as if she was continuing to use drugs just to hurt us. At some point I remember feeling that if I loved her differently then she would have had enough motivation to come out of her addiction sooner but this was long before I recognized it as a disease and the journey it would take for her to get well, if ever.

It would take a long time for us to understand that although it was her choice to begin to smoke crack it was not her body's choice to become addicted to it. I had to recognize it for the disease that it had become in order for me to remove the personal judgment and continue to love her for the mother figure she had always been to me. Once we backed off from pressuring her to change we began to notice that she was slowly coming around for HERSELF. She ultimately had to hit her own rock bottom before it started to make sense for her. Our role was to be there during the lowest of lows as well as the highest of highs so that we could be the perfect examples of love; comprised of support, consistency, honesty, compassion, and the desire to want more for the next person even when they feel they've reached their highest level of achievement or personal development.

My expectations of others have also changed in regards to what I feel how one should conduct their lives. It is a fact that everyone's reality is shaped by elements such as their culture, the way they interpret their life experiences, and their resolved and unresolved issues. It is also a fact that some of us place expectations on others based on how we would react if presented with the same situations which is entirely unfair if we are to get to the root of a problem and help foster solutions that are unique for that individual. However, we can rest in the fact that our expectations of one another pale in comparison to what God expects of each of us. No matter what WE expect of ourselves and others, God has always expected and provided the means for us to achieve more. But that achievement is recognized when we help foster that belief amongst each other.

It costs us absolutely nothing to give an encouraging vote of confidence to someone. A simple "I believe in you" goes a lot further than asking "what would make you do such a thing?" The first phrase may insinuate to someone that although you do not know the magnitude of their struggle you believe that they have what it takes, including your support, to weather the storm. The latter phrase implies extreme judgment and sometimes insult at a time where some may be emotionally susceptible. The latter phrase may also push someone to make more extreme decisions because they feel that no one cares or understands. You have a choice of whether or not to be on the team that creates support.

I am no stranger to passing unjust judgment myself. I had to learn that the level of condemnation that I leveled upon others for their actions is directly related to my own actions that can also be judged just as harshly without consideration of all related circumstances. Also, with judgment comes time and thoughts wasted on ideals that, again, have nothing to do with us. When we respect the walk of another, be it their footprints or future steps, we silently welcome the greatest results of their struggles yet to come while applauding the fight it took for them to get there. There should be a shift that results in less focus on the actions, which can be viewed as the EFFECT, and more focus on the reasons behind the actions. The best of our help can be made more effective when we attempt to understand the "BECAUSE" that results in the "WHY" of all of our actions.

Going back to the history with my aunt and her drug abuse I now believe wholeheartedly that had we paid more attention to the disease of addiction itself and not our personal judgment of the disease that we could have been more effective in her healing process that would have resulted in a much stronger support system that may have given her an increased feeling of security thereby possibly making her recovery process much more effective. Maybe we would have had the pleasure of having her loving presence with us much longer. Having walked a mile her shoes showed me that until I am able to understand the depth of one's decisions, which includes the history of behavior and experiences, I am ill-equipped to judge and that I would more than likely do more harm than good.

I want you to think back to a moment that you felt either pre-judged or misjudged for an action that you felt you were forced to take given the circumstances at the time. Wouldn't it have felt nice for someone to just ask "why" instead of jumping to conclusions without knowing all of the facts? That simple question can open doors to discovery that otherwise would have remained silent. I've witnessed people come alive once I made myself available to a better understanding of their situation. In fact, there have been cases whereby simply asking "why" allowed them to hear their own thought process and allowed them to answer their own concerns. By helping to validate their ability to think through a situation on their own I returned the power that they relinquished long ago; the ability to sometimes think through a situation and to exercise more positive solutions. Remember that sometimes we are forced to take certain actions because of how we interpret our available options. A less judgmental person may come along and present different options in a manner that feels less forced because at the end of the day they understand that the only responsibility they have is to present the options in a positive way. If those options aren't exercised then it isn't taken personally. The truth is that the options are always in the back of one's mind and we may find that the person exercised the option later on when it felt right for them to do so. Our work as a healthy member of one's support team should have no expiration date because we all receive what is important us at different times. What matters is that we receive it in time enough to for it to have the most positive and profound effect upon our healing process.

CHAPTER 16

PAYING IT FORWARD & DEFINING YOUR LEGACY

> ***Personal Pledge:*** *I understand that my goodwill and desire to help others become more successful will continue to create a multitude of positive connections. These connections will continue to share their positive energy on my behalf.*

This chapter is dedicated to the unconditional and unwavering love that was shown to me by my dearly departed paternal grandmother and aunt. I will always remember and honor them as two of my three mothers and as the primary forces that helped shape my belief that humility and grace are the cornerstone to a meaningful life. I will also remember them for their high level of compassion and knowing when to insert themselves in the lives of others during their time of need. For that, I am grateful for the pleasure of knowing and loving them and I will forever be inspired to help others achieve their personal best no matter what that may be. Their legacy is intact and it is through their legacy that I've learned the importance of living in a manner that will positively influence how you will be remembered once your time on this earth expires.

I want to go back to August 18, 2008. I was sitting on an airplane returning home to Maryland from after attending the memorial services held for my Aunt Brenda. She left this world at the young age 56, but I am so happy that I had the honor of receiving the fullness of her love and dedication. Her pain was over but her absence left an empty space within the pit of my soul and I debated whether or not to continue writing this book because my spirit had been so overwhelmingly exhausted. I was in the throes of a deep depression that virtually no one knew about and I was again questioning my reason for writing this book. I was also challenging my own gift; the very thing that God had bestowed upon me. I realized that even if I choose not to continue writing based on my original purpose I should continue because this was what she would have wanted me to do. I told her that I was in the process of writing this book before she passed and we discussed what I had hoped to talk about and she gave me her blessing. She had been one of my biggest supporters and always believed in my tenacity and my desire to help others.

I remember several years ago my mother telling me that I should always take the opportunity to use my blessings to bless someone else. My problem was that I felt that my situations at the time did not warrant me to believe that I was being blessed nor that I had anything to offer anyone. Like most of us, we disregard much of what our parents or elders tell us until we become mature enough to understand the significance of those teachings. I had to take myself out of the picture to understand the full context of that important statement. I never expected to feel such immense satisfaction by simply giving helpful advice or assistance to others who are now in predicaments that are similar to those that I faced at some time or another. I also realized that I was effectively building a positive legacy.

Let's define legacy for the purpose of this discussion. Merriam-Webster defines legacy as "something transmitted by or received from an ancestor or predecessor or from the past". Something has to be left behind or given to someone in order for it to constitute the start of a legacy. This definition does not equate legacy to being either positive or negative so there is always n opportunity for one to consciously decide what it is that they hope to leave behind for others. An example of a damaging legacy is if someone is remembered solely by their criminal acts or anything that paints a negative portrait. Examples of a positive legacy may consist of monetary donations, great literature, a speech that moves people to positive social change, or simply doing something kind for someone in hopes that they bestow the same personal generosity to someone else.

Most of us will fall into the latter of the categories previously mentioned. Performing a good deed for someone can be of no cost to you but may bring someone else a wealth of peace and serve as a wonderful example of faith, determination, and resilience. I have never met a single human being that does not have the capability to inspire someone else. With that being said, I believe that we all have an opportunity to use our story for the greater good of those that have yet to create the bridge between hurt and healing.

Every human being has either dealt with or currently dealing with some type of adversity. That single connection makes us all prone to receiving positive information and good deeds that can benefit our situation. Also, your ability to overcome any issue qualifies you as what I'd like to call a "crisis advocate" one that has tools beneficial to a specific issue that can help others overcome the same or similar crises. As a crisis advocate you can employ the use of advice and/or resources in various forms to help someone else with the hope that they carry the torch of performing good deeds. Your rebound from a fall can translate into the beginning of a successful climb for someone else.

How many times have you thought about the legacy that you leave behind? Do you honestly know, or care to know, how you would be remembered while you are here as well as when your expiration date has been reached? Not many of us actively participate in this thought process because it can be a little unnerving but can serve as the perfect catalyst for us put things in perspective and offers us a more conceptual look at the impact that our lives can have upon others. I firmly believe that our presence in this life manifests itself upon others in ways that we can't even imagine so we should all learn to take more control of the energy we project. We should also take notice as to how having an elevated level of confidence can be used as a platform for positive change for someone else.

I was able to learn valuable lessons about confidence, self-esteem, achievement, and peace by observing others in action and opening myself up to receive their gift. My grandfather and stepfather proved to be the finest examples of caring and loving men. They treated me as their own even when I may have not been as gracious and appreciative as I am now. I could almost do no wrong in my grandfather's eyes and to this day I am so thankful for his quiet and moving spirit. My stepfather chose to help my mother raise her children as his own without question. To him we are and will always be family. I admire him greatly and I make it a point to tell him when I feel it is necessary. He assisted me in making me feel comfortable in expressing my emotions while most men in my family struggled with the concept of emotional availability. Even when I was not in a position to understand these lessons I was able to receive them and store them for recall when the lesson was needed. Most times they were unaware of what they were doing and that I was even paying attention. Sometimes I didn't even realize that I was even paying attention but I found that my mind would recall things as if they were subconsciously planted there. I am not sure if some of these individuals had hoped they would inspire me but they were living examples of what I hoped to achieve and they allowed me to act as a parasite to their manifestation of positive energy. In turn, they were building their legacy. They were effectively positioning themselves to be remembered in the most positive manner. We all have this capability and I feel that it is our duty to pass on those great lessons that we either learned on our own or from others.

At age fourteen was when I had decided that all of my children were going to be adopted. I recall looking out of the kitchen window of my grandparent's home and deciding that I would have four children and that I would adopt all of them. I didn't flinch at the decision and it set the tone for what was to become one of my greatest motivations to becoming a successful human being. At that time I did not understand the motive or inspiration behind this declaration but I knew in my heart that part of my purpose included adopting children that were in need of a stable home and to provide those things that I felt I may have been deprived of as a child. It wasn't until I was in my mid-twenties that I realized some of the actions that played a part in this decision. My grandfather, along with my grandmother and aunt, raised me from my earliest memories and until I was a teenager. My grandfather was the epitome of a father-figure in my eyes and I yearned to one day fill the same shoes he wore. Also, my stepfather helped my mom raise four children that were not of his blood but whom he treated as his own. I had realized that everything that inspired me to adopt came from these positive male role models in my life. Maybe adoption was my way of "paying it forward" in their honor.

We all have the capability of passing on every positive tool that we've learned about ourselves to someone else whose spirit may be plagued with dilemmas or other elements that serve as blockades to their success. In fact, my primary focus for writing this book was to pass on great jewels of learning that I felt would help create a pivotal change in the lives of whom I am able to touch. People often feel alone in their problems until they come across someone who can say with all honesty that they understand and possibly have walked a few steps in that person's shoes. While overcoming your situation you've created a personal roadmap that is laden with methods of prevention, layers of determination, and knowledge that can be applied to almost any situation over and over again. This roadmap is the perfect gift to someone else. The greatest thing about this is that the roadmap can be distributed as many times as possible without losing its value. You never run out of inventory, and your life is attached to. You will be remembered for this gift and it can be given any day of the year without expiration. This is exciting to me because we have the ability to walk this earth with such immense information for trade.

An additional benefit of using your gift to help someone else is that you will come to understand that your adversities were not suffered in vain. You are now giving each situation a positive purpose and with that comes more control over the influence that these situations will provide to your life overall. This is when you truly come to understand that everything really does happen for a reason even if you don't understand it for sometimes several years after the fact. I can confidently say that every adversity served a function in my life and I would not be the same had I not experienced each and every one of them. I, like yourself, will no longer live with feelings of regret or pity and will find strength in healing and helping.

Part of the paying it forward process involves paying attention and listening for opportunities to inject positive energy into someone else's life. It doesn't always have to be in the form of advice but can exist through a donation of time or resources. I remember growing up with my mother and there were times where we may not have had enough to eat for holidays such as Christmas and Thanksgiving. We would receive donations of food and gifts from a local catholic church that always seem to come right on time. My siblings and I were unaware of how they knew that we were in need but we were still highly grateful nonetheless. Years later I still remember answering the door and receiving their thoughtful and amazing gifts. It was a gesture of extreme kindness because not only did they give us valuable resources but they also gave their time to make sure that we received the gift in our home and in our hands. I can also remember the feeling of inclusion because someone thought enough of our family to include us in their positive thoughts. It is a great feeling when someone genuinely gives a cares even when they may not personally know you. I will never forget those moments of charity because I am permanently inspired to be as charitable as I can.

Your life lessons can open doors of revelation for others and can provide the vehicle that elicits further positive change. You may not hear a "thank you" for every act of kindness you bestow upon someone but I can guarantee you that it will move others to repay the debt to someone else. This means that one kind gesture can spawn hundreds, thousands, or millions of additional kind gestures. In fact, in can create a movement. We see it portrayed in the media and in local communities and it serves as inspiration and highlights the sentiment that kind deeds should be performed with the least expectation of it being paid back to you. Do it because you can, you should, and because it makes you feel good as a person to do so. This does not mean to allow others to take advantage of that kindness. It should be tempered with some intention of a particular goal such as feeding a hungry family or helping an elder neighbor with house repairs.

I want to take a moment to discuss the positive value we can create when we decide to take on the rewarding challenge of mentoring. I previously mentioned my love for writing and how it helped my self-esteem during my school-aged years. My talent was recognized by very open-minded instructors and they gave of their time and energy to help me develop my passion. Overall, I felt important and recognized. I also felt that they wanted the best for me even when I didn't even know what my best could be. That's what mentoring is all about. It provides you the opportunity to form a trusting relationship with someone and offer guidance and encouragement in hopes of helping transform their lives for the better. Children, adults, and families can all benefit from mentoring and it can be applied to any area of life such as business and education.

You may be an expert painter and are able to recognize someone that has vast potential in the same area. Now, you have the ability to motivate someone else by sharing your story of struggle and triumph as well as offering invaluable advice that will undoubtedly assist them in achieving their goals. Your life story can serve as the bridge that connects you to the hearts of others. For example, I am at a point in my life where my issues associated with sexual abuse, unprovoked violence, and abandonment have not hampered my desire to open myself enough to share my experience in as positive a way that I can. I not only speak of the incidents. I also speak of the importance of being resilient and learning what makes you the individual in which you were created to be. I may never know how many lives will be touched by my revelations but I will touch those that are meant to be touched by my stories and I require no specific form of gratitude except that these efforts are passed on to others if at all possible.

Be prepared for the fact that everyone you wish to help may not be ready to receive it. Do not let that prevent you from trying to help someone more than once. I had to learn how not to be pushy in my efforts to attempt to help others overcome adversity, especially when they haven't acknowledged that a problem even exists. The period of denial is when you may meet the most resistance to your kind act of sharing of information and experience. Either they feel that they can handle the problem on their own or embarrassed to admit that a problem exists. That's why I find it imperative to help the person find some type of familiarity by sharing your situation. As they say, experience is the best teacher. Your experience in overcoming adversity prepares you to become an instructor for success and that power is extremely great as well as positively contagious.

Usually, one has to hit some sort of bottom before a problem is acknowledged. It is at this point where the realization begins and the opportunity to assist is more readily accepted. That does not mean that we wait for this to happen. It means that we understand the realistic process that is involved and are not deterred by the resistance. I usually make small acknowledgements by stating my support in unobvious ways. Then, I continue to pay attention in hopes of recognizing those opportunities to interject more support. By the time the bottom falls out I have already laid the foundation that makes it less difficult for the person to recognize my offering of assistance.

During my darkest moments of coming to grips with my sexual abuse I remember feeling so alone and confused because the only person I knew that understood what I was feeling had been virtually ignored by our family as if the problem never existed. I slowly began to realize that I was not alone in this and that countless other families had been stricken with this type of betrayal. I remember watching a broadcast of Oprah Winfrey one day and one of her guests was an NFL star who had recently published a book detailing his struggle with sexual abuse. He had explained that his goal was to help others overcome similar situations. I was very moved by this because most men cower at the revelation that they were sexually violated. But, once a purpose is attached to something it makes it so much less difficult to share because the main concern is achievement of the end result. Sometimes, our purpose for going through and coming out of adversity is to simply pay it forward.

The act of paying it forward shows your honest desire to improve the quality of life for someone else. It also provides the vehicle that makes you feel good internally and feeds your spirit something that it needs to proceed with an increased sense of purpose. There is an immeasurable amount of satisfaction and joy that is experienced when you feel that you've made a positive impact on someone else's life.

Paying it forward is can also be used as your means of honoring those that have had a positive influence over your own personal development. Some of us can proudly say that we may have learned a valuable lesson from a caring parent, aunt, uncle, teacher, or even a passer-by that felt that it was his or her duty to give you the attention that they felt you deserved. Well, now is a perfect time to honor their gift by giving that gift to someone else who is equally as deserving as you were at that point in time. No one says that you have to be the perfect person in order to pass on jewels of wisdom, experience, and newfound lessons with a graciousness that does not require a "thank you". You just have to be the type of person who wants to be remembered for the good work that you chose to do.

Our words are the promises that create the outline of our character while our deeds provide the color that determines the opinions of our results. Our intentional deeds of good will have the potential to save lives, bring people closer to God, and hopefully persuade those that have been blessed by our work to bless others. We all have the ability to smile in the face of adversity even when the odds are not in our favor. We sometimes forget the magnitude of small acts of kindness and how they can inspire others to follow suit. Had it not been for the generous hearts and minds that have traversed my life I probably would not have been inspired to write this book because most of the intent is found in my need to honor them by passing some of the lessons on to you. One of my hopes is that your spirit becomes softer and kinder as you grow closer to understanding who you are and your inherit potential for greatness. I also hope you begin to live your life with a more charitable spirit and are moved to give of yourself whenever possible. Every event in life provides an opportunity for learning. It is those same events that provide the spiritual connectivity to someone else that helps to make room for life-sustaining balance, purpose, and uniqueness.

CAPSTONE QUESTIONAIRE

You have finally come to the end of this journey with what I hope is a heightened sense of self-awareness as it relates to your personal value and your right overall happiness. This questionnaire was designed to afford you the opportunity to begin thinking more robustly about yourself, the contributions that you are able to bestow upon the world, and the positive affect that your life can have upon others.

I provided no space for written answers because I feel it is best for you to allow the answers to live within your spirit. Answer each question back to yourself as if you are not only the reader but also your very own audience. By doing this you will begin to trust YOUR voice a little more and better understand the power of your own thoughts and how they affect your next move.

Final Personal Pledge: *I finally understand that love, adoration, admiration, achievement and celebration must begin with me. I also understand that there is power in the declaration of what I desire for myself and what I desire to bestow upon the world. I can now imagine my best life regardless of the condition of the world in which it is lived.*

1. In your opinion, why is important for one to understand and accept their ENTIRE LIFE STORY as it relates to healing emotional wounds?

2. Taking your whole life into consideration do you feel comfortable enough to accept your entire truth as it is instead of how you had HOPED it would have been?

3. Are there any events or periods of time that you find more difficult to accept? If so, why?

4. What are some of the truths about your life and yourself that may have been initially too difficult to accept but are now easier to recognize and accept?

5. Looking back at all of the adversities/situations that you have faced or currently facing do you understand the purpose of each situation and the difference between "going through" and "coming through"?

6. Now that you have a better understanding of the meaning and power of forgiveness how will it affect your quality of life to be able to once and for all forgive your past knowing that it has already transpired and cannot be either unwritten or rewritten?

7. Are you able to recognize how much of your future is still controlled by your past as a result of not forgiving?

8. Are you able to forgive YOURSELF for dreams yet achieved, wrong-doings against others, and other situations that you feel you may have had a negative contribution to your current quality of life.

9. Having enacted forgiveness on multiple levels are there any relationships that you would like to repair? If so, how has forgiveness allowed you to move forward with those efforts?

10. If given the opportunity how would you explain forgiveness, and the benefits of its use, to others?

11. One benefit of self-forgiveness is that it allows one to experience a higher level of self-love. If asked, how would you explain the importance and benefits of self-love to someone else?

12. How would you explain the correlation between the lack of self-love and one's level of self-esteem?

13. Why is it oftentimes dangerous to seek validation in specific situations, especially in personal and romantic situations?

14. How has your level of self-esteem directly affected your choices as it pertains to relationships? Is it possible that some of these relationships may not have ever come to pass if your self-esteem was at a higher level at that time?

15. If you have been so fortunate enough to discover your true purpose (reason for existence) how do you hope to utilize your Godly-bestowed gifts to influence others?

16. How would you explain to someone the value of accepting one's purpose?

17. What is the message that you hope that your fulfillment of purpose leaves upon those that you encounter?

18. Are you aware of the energy that you exude when you enter a room? Is it filled with confidence, self-doubt, arrogance, or discomfort?

19. Do you believe that your actions have greater control over the initial perception that most will have of you?

20. How important is your presentation to others as it relates to your goals and aspirations?

21. Do you feel that at times your career and/or personal life may have somehow been hindered as a result of how you represented yourself to others? If so, how would you change your presentation while still being true to who you are?

22. If so, what changes can you think of that will increase your chances of being taken seriously and better understood?

23. Do you feel that you are prepared to do what is necessary to begin to achieve the goals that you have set forth for yourself? If so, what do you feel is required for you to successfully complete these goals?

24. How important is a plan of action as it relates to taking the steps necessary to fulfill your goals?

25. Are you prepared to not only recover from setbacks and shortfalls but are you also prepared to learn the valuable lessons that each may provide?

26. Can you list at least two people who are willing to serve on your support team that will provide accountability and encouragement?

27. As it relates to support system, how important is it to recognize who comprises your support system?

28. If one was to consider becoming a part of your support system are you able to effectively communicate exactly what is required of them?

29. In turn, are you in a position to offer the same support to someone else if needed? If not, why?

30. Expectations are important and required of ALL relationships. Are you comfortable in communicating your expectations to others when necessary? If not, why?

31. As it relates to romantic relationships why is it important to communicate expectations sooner rather than later?

32. While reviewing past situations are there any instances whereby effectively communicating your expectations may have led to more positive results?

33. If you are a parent or guardian of a child what type of life do you envision for them and how will your current behavior influence their future behavior?

34. Considering the previous question, what behaviors do you feel require modification in order to become the finest role model to those whom you have may have major influence over?

35. If you had the opportunity to speak to a roomful of people about understanding and living with positive intent what would be the main point of your discussion?

36. How can your victory over your past adversities be of service to others who are or may experience similar situations?

37. How would you explain the purpose and benefits of forgiveness to someone who may be struggling with the process?

38. How do you hope to be remembered by those whose paths you may come across?

39. While taking a survey of your personal characteristics what is one or some of the most valuable traits that you feel will stand out positively to anyone you may encounter?

40. Do you fully understand that as God's child you were always qualified, created with validity, and expected to fulfill a divine purpose that is sometimes only revealed by the removal of adversity?

Final Thoughts & Wishes

"Beloved, I wish above all things that thou mayest prosper and be in health, even as thy soul prospereth."

(3 John 1:2, KJV)

      As you can see from the scripture quoted above, the promise of your right to prosperity in every aspect of your life was declared long before you were created. This right is shared by all of God's children, and therefore, no one is deemed more or worthy of greatness. By simply acknowledging that you are worthy of prosperity, you automatically unlock your capacity to reach YOUR pinnacle of excellence that has always been embedded within your entire being. Everything that makes you who you are was purposely planned, and it is up to you to take full advantage of the gifts and capabilities bestowed upon you. The ability to reach your full potential rests solely in your hands. While some segments of your journey will be challenging at times, accepting the truth of your self-worth shall re-energize your steps and fuel your movement forward in a positive way and allow you to rebound quicker. He expects nothing less than YOUR best, which is not to be compared to the best of anyone else. Do not allow the temperamental worldly opinion of your value to diminish your understanding that God recognizes and supports your strength, a strength that is based in faith and the belief that He will fortify the areas that He feels require His intervention.

      Your life has always been your greatest teacher. Avail yourself to the strength that awaits you at the end of each trial. That same strength will carry you through your next trial, which will then add an additional layer of strength and learning. At some point, you will realize that your armor is fully intact, and you are not only prepared for battle but you are also prepared to embrace new challenges. Enlighten those who are eager to learn from your journey, and transform your pain into power and purpose.

About Cory George, MS, CAMS-I, CDVS-I

mailto:Cory@RoughDraftMedia.com

Cory George is a graduate of Colorado Technical University and holds a Bachelor's Degree in Software Engineering and a Master's Degree in Management. In addition, George is also a Certified Anger Management Specialist – I, Certified Domestic Violence Specialist – I, coach, motivational speaker, and multimedia producer. His interest in writing began at the age of four as a means of alternative communication due to a severe speech impediment. By the age of seven he was composing short stories, songs, and one act plays. Now his writing is used as a vessel of information that fosters inspiration, self-awareness, and personal improvement. *Sit or Stand* 2.0 is very much a labor of love and a realization of the power of determination, self-empowerment, the acceptance of God's presence in one's life, and the value of creating a healthy environment suitable for creating and attaining specific life goals.

As a documentarian, he is the producer of the highly acclaimed **Whispers in the Night: The Journey Back to the Light** which serves as one of the most candid conversations the full life-cycle of childhood sexual assault as told from the point-of-view of three black male survivors. His next documentary, tentatively titled *Daddy* is currently in production.

A native of Houston, Texas and Ville Platte, Louisiana, he currently resides in Washington, DC with his two sons, Tyler and Justin.

Sit or Stand 2.0

www.ingramcontent.com/pod-product-compliance
Lightning Source LLC
Chambersburg PA
CBHW021942290426
44108CB00012B/932